TURNING JAPANESE

MAZDA 110S

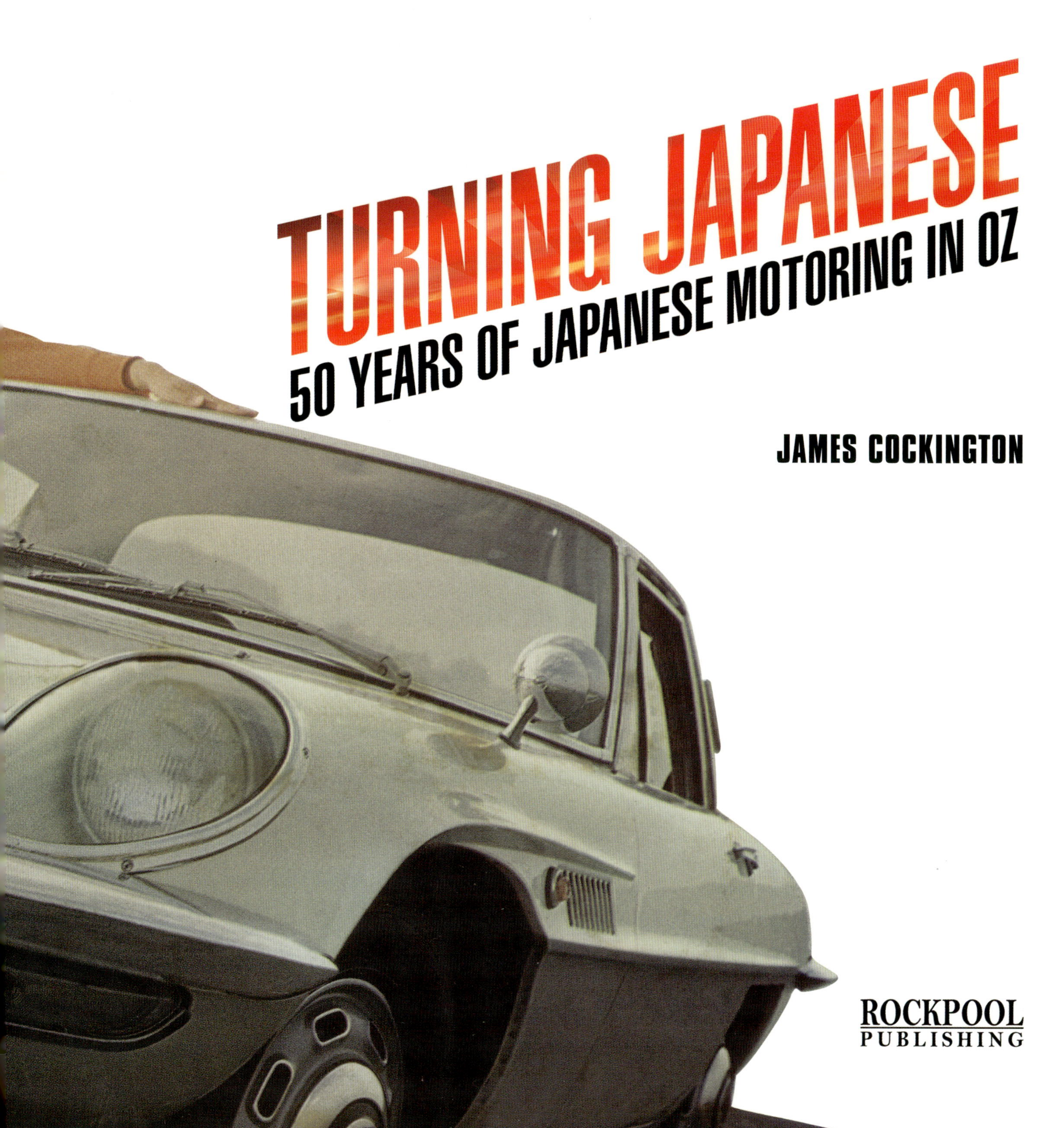
TURNING JAPANESE
50 YEARS OF JAPANESE MOTORING IN OZ
JAMES COCKINGTON
ROCKPOOL
PUBLISHING

TOYOTA 2000GT
ESSO
2000GT

CONTENTS

WRX

LIQUI MOLY
NISSAN
nismo
35A
NISSAN
ICOM

BB-100
PENRITH MAZDA
60
Daily Mirror
DUNLOP

AEI·518

Classic Japanese

It's no secret that the Japanese classic car movement is booming. After taking off as a minority cult activity a few decades ago, some cars have already increased in value by as much as five times. This includes exotics like the Honda S600 but also, surprisingly, the first series of Toyota Corollas in good condition.

Opinions vary but the Japanese classics now considered most desirable include the Mazda R100, Datsun Fairlady, Datsun 2000, Datsun 1600 SSS (especially rally cars), EXA Turbos and the first series of Toyota Celicas and Crowns. The really valuable ones are the limited editions, including some that were never sold in Australia but have since been imported.

We've concentrated mainly on the rarities, especially those produced in the 1960s and 1970s when the Japanese invasion was at its peak in Australia. We've sourced a lot of rare photos in the files of *Racing Car News*

magazine, along with some classic road and track tests.

This was a fascinating period when these cars — still treated with suspicion by many locals — first started to make a big impact.

'You'd be surprised at just what's around in Australia,' says Brett Wild, president of the Bellett Car Club of Victoria and an authority on Japanese classics.

'Not only nice cars but some bloody rare stuff too, both in what was imported when

DAVID SELDON
6
GOODYEAR

DANE
41
West End
mazda
RACING CAR NEWS
GOOD YEAR

TOSHIBA
NISSAN
36
ICOM
ICOM
TOSHIBA
TOSHIBA
Steadfast
MACK
MACK

new and what's been imported privately.' He knows of examples of the Toyota 2000GT, KGC10 Skyline GTR, Nissan GT-R, Mazda Cosmo, Nissan Sylva, and factory race cars such as Prince Skylines, Belletts, Celicas, Mazda RX3s, Corollas, Mitsubishis and Datsuns.

New ones keep on turning up. One rumour is that some Datsun SSS two-doors were sent to Australia by mistake and were sold off rather than being shipped back. And a lot of interesting machinery was imported as one-offs to test the market, some of which has survived.

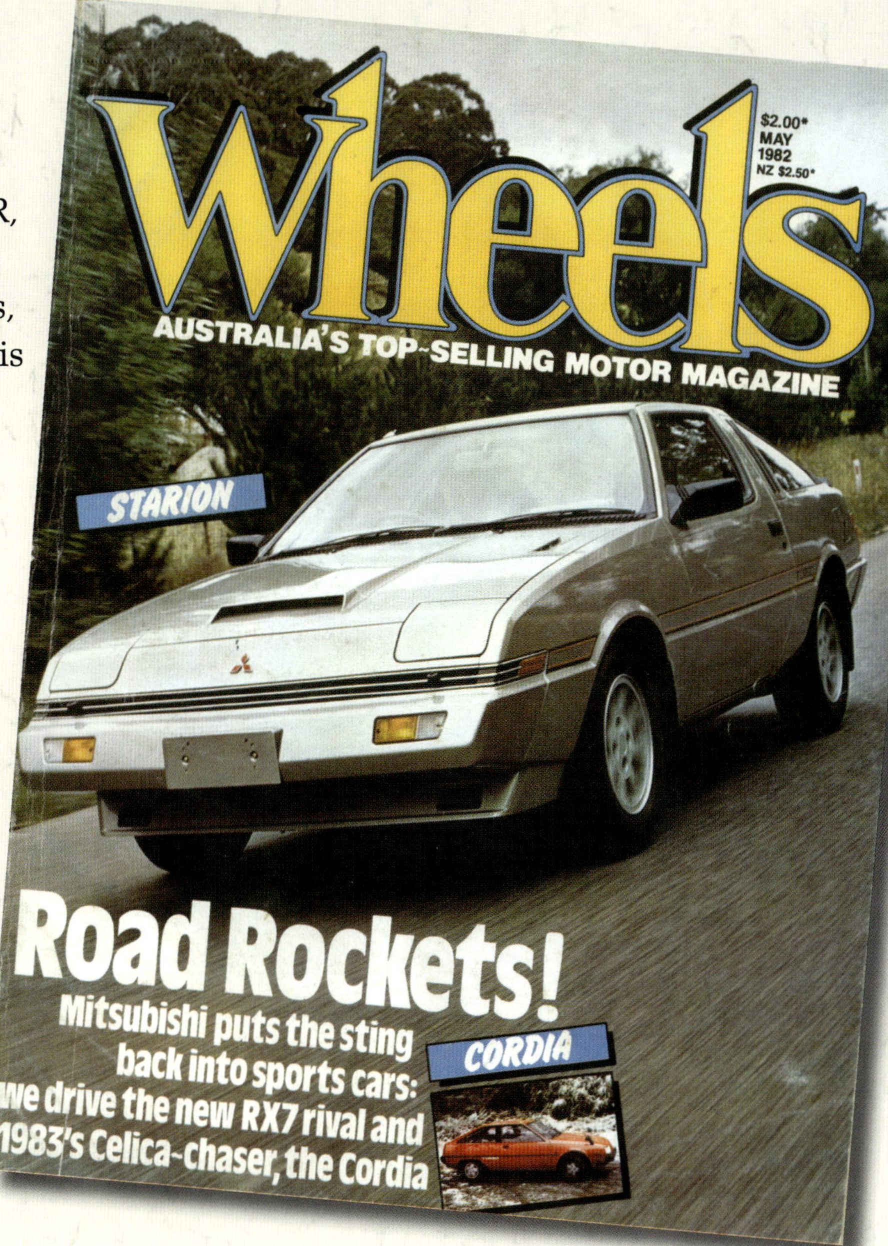

Australia is a great place to source these cars, better than Japan in some cases. Strict rego rules in Japan mean that most old cars have been scrapped long ago. Good examples are also hard to find elsewhere in the world. In Europe, the salt used on the roads in winter mean that far less cars have survived. In America, most were converted to left-hand drive, not always professionally.

The Japanese car club scene is growing every year. When they hold a show they usually have around 300 to 400 cars on display. There isn't the Ford versus Holden rivalry you find at Australian-made shows and everyone seems to enjoy each other's choice of car, whatever the make and model.

It's a movement that will only get stronger in the future.

The Start of the REVOLUTION

Two young men standing proudly

... in front of the offices of the Toyota Motor Sales Co Ltd hold a unique place in Australian automotive history. In 1957, they sailed from Japan to Australia with their car, officially known as a Toyopet Crown.

Those pioneers comprised the first Japanese team to compete in the Mobilgas Trial, an endurance event that took them around Australia. Starting in Melbourne on 21 August 1957, they did a 9000-mile

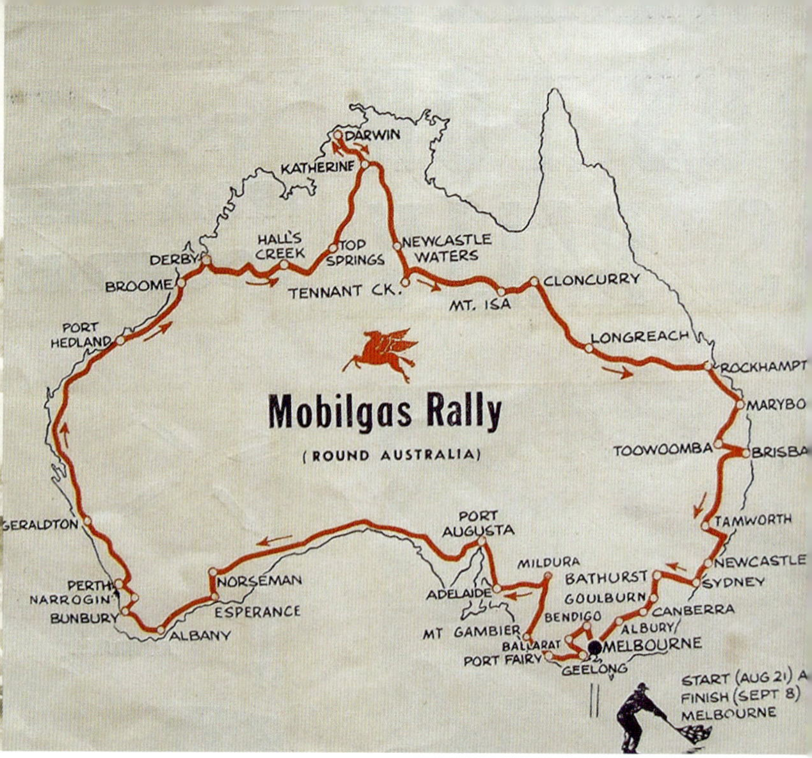

(14 500-km) loop of the continent in a clockwise direction, arriving back in Melbourne on 8 September.

It has been claimed that they were the first Japanese to compete in any international sporting event since World War II. That's not quite true – the previous year a Japanese team competed at the Olympic Games held in Melbourne and won four gold medals. Nevertheless, the Japanese were

This page The Toyota competing in the1957 Mobilgas rally .
Opposite At the draw for starting positions for the Mobilgas Rally in 1958, a Toyopet Crown was up on stage along with a Hillman and a Fiat.

not welcome visitors to Australia for many years after the war. Up until the mid-1960s there were reports of locals spitting on the windscreens of Japanese cars at pedestrian crossings. It's worth noting that the route of the 1957 Mobilgas Trial passed through Darwin, the city which Japanese fighter planes had bombed only 15 years earlier.

With the help of an Australian navigator, Toyota's team finished the event. The management in Japan must have been happy. The next year, three new Toyopet

AUSTRALIA
JAPAN
100

Crowns entered the Mobilgas Trial. The cars were colour-coded in white with contrasting panels of aqua, red and navy blue – one was prominently featured in the GTV Nine studios at the televised draw for starting positions. All three Crowns failed to finish, two rolling and the third retiring after hitting a kangaroo.

Nissan also entered two Datsuns in the 1958 Mobilgas Trial. Both finished and the car driven by Y Namba and K Okuyama came in 25th outright, winning the smallest class for cars under 1000 cc.

It was clear that the Japanese manufacturers were beginning to see Australia as a potential market for their range of automobiles and trucks.

DATSUN: THE EARLY YEARS

A 1959-model Datsun Bluebird 1200, code-named the P310, was displayed at the 1960 Melbourne Motor Show. It was an unremarkable-looking car but one to take notice was Laurence 'Larry' Hartnett, the former managing director of GM-H. Sniffing an opportunity, he flew to Tokyo and secured the rights to sell Datsuns in Australia.

The first shipment of 100 Bluebirds arrived in December 1960. Initial sales were sluggish. The revised P311 Bluebird, launched in 1961, attracted more interest thanks to a more powerful engine, putting out a respectable 60 bhp at 5000 rpm. The car had a reputation for being tough and reliable, if not exactly exciting to drive.

One of the first dealerships to sell the car was Capitol Motors, based in William Street, Sydney's glittering mile of car showrooms. Capitol sold 132 Bluebirds in 1961 out of a total of 514 sold nationwide. Once a Queensland distributor was established, more were sold in that state than any other.

It was a promising start. But nobody could have predicted how quickly the Japanese would be up there taking on the big boys.

Arnold Glass, boss of Capitol Motors, was a noted racer, He entered a three-car team of Bluebirds in the 1962 Bathurst Six-Hour Classic, the first endurance race for production cars to be held at the Mount Panorama circuit. Entered in the class for the cheapest cars, they surprised many with their speed down Conrod Straight.

'They were really rapid,' Mike Kable reported in *Sports Car World*, 'and one car in the team was pushed to 100 mph [161 km/h] on one lap, while the others consistently recorded better than 90 mph.' But that was until their standard wheels and brake drums began to fracture under the strain. Arnold Glass finished eighth in class after several stops for repairs.

By 1963 the car was popular enough to be the subject of a 'Know Your Datsun Bluebird' article in *Modern Motor* magazine.

Teams from Datsun and Toyota again took part in the 1964 Round Australia trial, this time sponsored by Ampol. Toyota entered four current-model Crowns, including a works team car driven by Shihomi Hosoya and Masaharu Terao.

Later that year, two factory Datsun Bluebirds ran in the first Sandown Park Six-Hour race in Melbourne. These were the sporty 1300 SS models, entered by David McKay's Scuderia Veloce race team. The cars finished ninth and 11th outright.

Scuderia Veloce then entered a three-car Bluebird team in the 1965 Bathurst enduro, but the cars were withdrawn when their fragile wheels cracked during practice.

Above The Nissan Silva.

Sales were picking up after a tentative start. In 1964 Hartnett sold over 8000 Nissan/Datsun cars through its growing national network of dealers. These included the luxury Nissan Cedric, along with the new Datsun Fairlady sports car. A handful of the ultra-desirable Nissan Silvas were also imported. These stylish sports coupes, with bodywork designed in Italy, were later joined by the Prince Skyline 2000 GT, the most powerful model in Nissan's rapidly expanding product range, which featured three carburettors fitted as standard.

Nissan merged with its Japanese competitor, the Prince Motors Company, in 1966. Previously Prince cars had been sold in Australia by Wheelmar Motors, which had a Prince Gloria at the Sydney Motor Show as early as 1964: 'A single-overhead-cam, twelve port head with 105 bhp, three-speed synchro box with optional overdrive, finned drum brakes ...' noted *Racing Car News*. 'Might have possibilities.'

Once certain sales quotas had been met, government regulations required local manufacture, and in 1966 the first Australian-built Datsun, a cream-coloured 1300 sedan, rolled off the line at the Pressed Metal Corporation factory in Sydney. When they outgrew the PMC factory, Nissan took over Volkswagen's former assembly plant in the Melbourne suburb of Clayton.

It had taken Nissan just over five years to become established in Australia.

This page Victorian premier Sir Henry Bolte officially opened the new Nissan factory.

TOYOTA: THE PIONEER

Toyota had also seen the potential of the fast-growing Australian market and had begun local assembly three years earlier than Nissan through the Australian Motor Industries (AMI) group at their Port Melbourne plant.

The first Toyota to be built there was the Tiara, which was displayed at the 1963 Melbourne Motor Show. This model had a 1463 cc, 65 bhp motor, three-speed gearbox and independent front torsion bar suspension. The retail price was approximately £950. In their annual motor show report, *Modern Motor* suggested Toyota had a real future in Australia.

Toyota sedans, wagons and utilities were sold through the AMI dealer network. In the first year, 5720 units were sold but things really took off when the Crown and Corona models began to be assembled at Port Melbourne. The 1.5-litre Corona was an instant success – it was keenly priced and sold 7500 units in 1966. This marked the start of the first local sales battle between Nissan/Datsun and Toyota.

Left One of the three Toyopet Crowns competing in the 1964 Mobilgas Rally.

JUST ARRIVED! THE NEW

TOYOTA "TIARA"

We are proud to announce that we have been chosen as agents for this remarkable new car. Comfortable seating for five in a 65 hp 85 mph sedan which gives 45 mpg—all for only £915. Test drive now. See Gary Cooke.

COOKE AND SAVILLE

MOTORS Pty. Ltd.

12-14 Parramatta Rd., Flemington, N.S.W. UM 5666

13
13 A
QLD
PHJ·309

Datsun Bluebirds in one of the Surfers Paradise enduros in the late 1960s. The chap in number 13 seems to be enjoying himself …

My Fairlady

The arrival of the Datsun Fairlady in 1963 came out of the blue. Australians were getting used to Nissan producing cheap, solid, unremarkable vehicles, aimed at a mass market. So the first Japanese two-seater convertible seen here was a surprise.

Sports Car World magazine was impressed enough to feature it on the cover, and label it the 'Japanese Rival to MGB'. *SCW*'s tester Chris Beck was initially sceptical.

'The feeling was that BMC, Rootes and Australian Motor Industries (importers of the Triumph Spitfire) had the soft-top market tied up and another car – which on the surface seemed to offer no more or do its job any better – would not really sell well. After testing the car our opinions changed dramatically.' Beck believed the English manufacturers had a serious challenger.

As a bonus, the Fairlady looked good. Beck saw a similarity to the Fiat 1600 Cabriolet but after deliberation decided that the Datsun was probably an original.

NSW
AJG·444

The most startling thing was its performance. This first edition featured a pushrod 1488 cc in line four, yet Beck found that it hit the high 90s with ease, and was likely to exceed the magic ton —that's 100 mph (161 km/h) — under favourable conditions. Maximum speed in first was 30 mph, second was 47 mph, third 78 mph. He was unable to explore the limits in fourth.

'Staff members were most surprised at the way the car accelerated and the times it recorded through the quarter mile,' he said. His best was around 19.3 seconds; 0 to 60 mph took 14.4 seconds. 'During our acceleration runs, it was quite easy — although we avoided it — to wind the tacho needle off the clock and round to a point that must have corresponded to almost 7000 rpm.' When this happened — accidentally on purpose we assume — the only indication of stress was the exhaust note and the whine of the transmission.

Complaints from Chris Beck were mainly

to do with slowing the thing down. The Fairlady was fitted with four drum brakes, which tended to fade after a couple of hard pumps – discs on the front would have greatly improved driver confidence. Suspension was adequate at a time when sports cars were expected to give you a rough ride. Handling was reasonable, with initial understeer leading to controlled oversteer if pushed hard.

There was some body noise, again typical of the breed, but putting up the hood was a more serious annoyance. Chris Beck's best time for this task was 6 minutes 55 seconds. No wonder most owners opted for an aftermarket fibreglass hardtop that could be clicked on and off with relative ease. Beck

was also disappointed to find no oil pressure gauge was fitted.

Apart from these quibbles, the Fairlady stood up well against its competitors. Priced at £1265 in December 1963, it slotted into the gap in the market between the MGB and the Spitfire ... 'performance-wise there is no other sports car under 1500 cc imported in volume into this country which can touch it.'

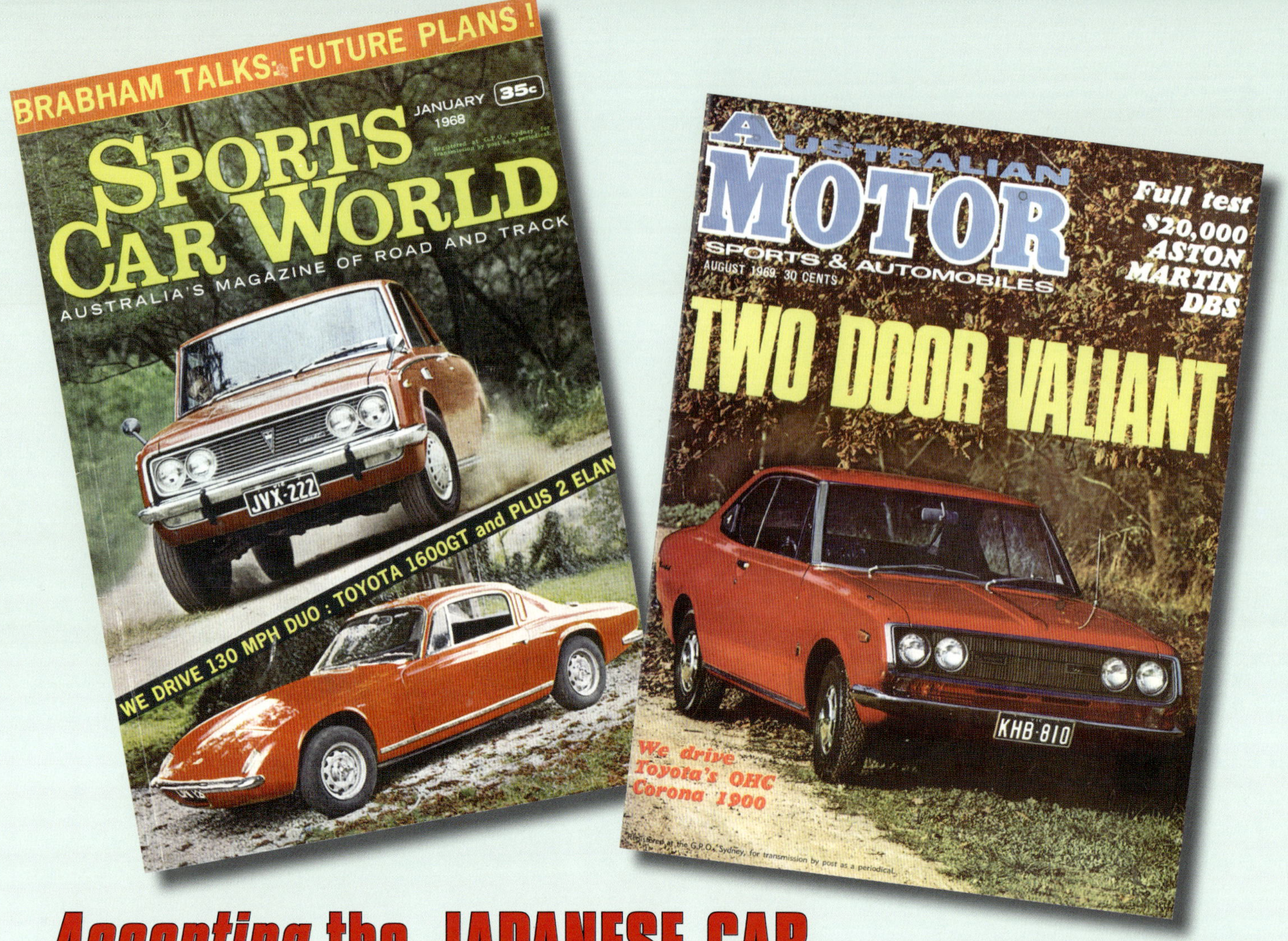

Accepting the JAPANESE CAR

The 1960s and there were still some Australians who resisted buying anything Japanese.

When AMI first flew a Japanese flag in front of their headquarters they received several letters of complaint from the public.

Regardless, by the mid-1960s Japanese cars were an accepted part of the Australian new car scene, featuring prominently at Bathurst and other races, as well as adorning the covers of car magazines. And the cars were selling in increasing quantities.

One indication of this is in the *Caltex Travel Fun Book*, aimed at keeping kids amused on long trips. The 1965 edition includes a spotting game. You were awarded points based on the cars' rarity. Holdens, Falcons and Valiants were the most common so only scored five. Datsuns and Toyotas were in the 10-point category, along with Volkswagens and Morris Minis. Nissans rated 15 points but were still more likely to be seen than a Studebaker (20 points), Mercedes Benz (25) or Rolls Royce (50).

The LIGHT BULB Car & *other oddities*

Among other Japanese cars to make their appearance in this fertile period was what must have been the first Subaru in Australia, a micro car powered by a 360 cc engine. One was on display at the Melbourne Motor Show in 1963, having been road-tested by *Modern Motor* that January. It impressed with its fuel economy and good handling, if not its styling. It looked as if it had been designed by Walt Disney for Minnie Mouse to drive.

A shipment of Mazda R360 minicars also arrived in 1963. Mazda commercial vehicles (panel vans and utes) were already imported, but the R360 was the first passenger car to be available. It was part of a short-lived fad for mini cars.

The Mazdas were even smaller than Bill Buckle's Australian-made fibreglass Goggomobil Darts. The R360 was powered by a 356 cc, 16 bhp, air-cooled, rear-mounted, four-stroke V2 engine, with a claimed 55-mph (88.5-km/h) maximum speed. Its price in Australia was around the £550 mark, tax paid. In comparison, the 1963 basic model EH Holden cost £1050 when it was released.

The microscopic Mazdas soon earned the nickname 'the light-bulb car,' a reference to a brand of light bulbs also known as Mazda. The joke was that a 50-watt globe put out more power that the R360 – possibly not far from the truth. These days you'll pay big money for one, as you would for one of the

first Subarus, or a Mitsubishi Minicar, also available here in the early 1960s.

Limited numbers of twin-cylinder Colt 600 and four-cylinder Colt 1000 cars were also sold, plus a handful of the Mitsubishi Debonair six-cylinder luxury cars.

WHAT'S NEW HERE

MAZDA coupe—two-seater from Japan, to sell here around £550 tax-paid.

The Sturt Griffith *tick* of Approval

HINO *Contessa*

Hino

The Hino Contessa is a Japanese car of character. Essentially it is a ruggedly constructed saloon of medium size which rides well over most surfaces and has a moderate performance, but a good top speed.

It adds another to the ranks of rear-engined cars, and in this case the power unit is a smooth and quiet four-cylinder delivering 55 horsepower, and driving through a three-speed gearbox with a column change. In the near future there will be an optional model, at a slightly higher price, having a four-speed box, a floor change and individual front seats.

The Contessa is a good-looking car. The body is styled by Michelotti of Italy, and the frontal and cabin treatment resembles his elegant Triumph 2000.

The boot is under the front bonnet and (for this arrangement) is reasonably spacious, with maximum measurements of 49 x 36 x 15in. There is also a small luggage well behind the rear seat, but of course rear-engined cars rarely have as much, or as well shaped, luggage space as the conventional design.

Observations

The car gives a first impression of solidity which is not dispelled by extensive testing. It feels, and is, a medium car which can be driven hard over rough going without demur or bottoming.

The interior is more spacious than usual in Japanese cars of this size, and rear kneeroom of 12 inches is good for any medium car. One penalty of a cabin disposed well forward is the intrusion of the front wheel arches into the front floor, but this is small price to pay for a compact turning circle of 30 feet.

The brakes are heavy by today's standards but they do stop the car straight and without rear-wheel locking, doubtless due to the engine weight over the rear wheels.

The long gearshift linkage to the gearbox in the rear is assisted by an electromagnetic selecting system. Its movements are conventionally light, and effective synchromesh is provided on all forward ratios. Some modification is necessary, however, to damp the vigorous whipping of the gearlever on rough roads, which regularly flips the selector into neutral.

Performance

The road performance of the Contessa is reasonably good, but any medium-sized engine performs better with a four-speed rather than a three-speed gearbox. The Contessa requires

CONTESSA PERFORMANCES	
MAXIMUM SPEEDS:	m.p.h.
Top gear:	82
Second	57.5
FUEL FACTS:	m.p.g.
Touring fuel consumption (at 42 m.p.h. over test route):	35.0
Ton-miles per gallon:	37.6
Fuel efficiency rating:	1595
ACCELERATION:	secs
0-50 m.p.h. through gears,	13.5
Second, 20-40 m.p.h.	6.7
" 30-50 "	7.8
Top, 20-40 "	15.0
" 30-50 "	15.0
" 40-60 "	16.5
HILL-CLIMBING:	m.p.h.
Lett River (1 in 12), in second:	40-53
Fitzgerald Mt. (1 in 11), in second:	30-45

26

Nine Japanese models were included in the January 1966 edition of *Sturt Griffith's Road Tests*, the annual magazine produced by the *Sydney Morning Herald*'s respected motoring expert. They made up a quarter of the 27 new models Griffith had tested the previous year.

'One might say that the greatest single development in 1965 has been the Japanese invasion,' he wrote. 'Almost every week has revealed something new from Japanese factories, and while cars of this nationality have not yet gained a large percentage of the overall Australian sales, they have certainly shaken the complacency of Australian manufacturers and distributors.'

Examples tested by him in 1965 were the Toyota Corona and Crown, Datsun Fairlady, Honda S600, Isuzu Bellett 1500, Mazda 800 (the estate version), Prince Gloria and Skyline plus — a real rarity — the rear-engined four-cylinder Hino Contessa with bodywork by Michelotti. These days Hino is better known as a maker of trucks.

Griffith was reasonably impressed by the Contessa, describing it as a 'ruggedly constructed saloon of medium size which rides well over most surfaces and has a moderate performance but a good top speed' — 82 mph (132 km) to be specific.

The version he drove was a three-speed manual with a column change. Soon after a significantly improved four-on-the-floor version became available for a slightly higher price. The engine was a 1250 cc four, liquid cooled, with a hemispherical head and twin-throat Hitachi carburettor. The car tested was supplied by the distributors, Eastern Motor Corporation Pty Ltd.

All the cars were tested by Griffith over the same 250-mile course, from Lawson in the Blue Mountains to Bathurst and Orange, returning via Blayney. The route included high-speed laps of the Mount Panorama and Gnoo Blas (Orange) race circuits, with detours to include dirt tracks and steep hills. Brakes were tested with a series of 12 emergency stops from 60 mph (96.5 km) on a quiet section of highway.

Some of the cars performed better than others, but overall Sturt Griffith saw the enormous potential in this emerging market. 'Having seen the major Japanese factories at work, and discussed technical developments with their designers, I would broadly assess Japanese cars as well finished and exceptionally well equipped – if not technically advanced.'

There was one notable stand-out.

Griffith was especially impressed by the technical advancement of the Honda S600, which he described as an outstanding small

Above The Isuzi 1600 Florian, launched in late 1967.

THIS CAR
12/12 WARRANTY
BELLETT
is
• FASTER
• STRONGER
• MORE ECONOMICAL
• BETTER FINISHED
AND HUNDREDS OF POUNDS CHEAPER THAN ANY CAR IN ITS CLASS!!!
PROVE IT... DRIVE ONE!
BE A SPORT-DRIVE A BELLETT
Bellett 1500
Yours from as little as
73/- weekly
ONLY £950 TAX PAID
• 4-speed synchro-mesh transmission; 4 cylinders; overhead valves.
• Acceleration—do the standing quarter-mile in under 19 seconds.
• 4-wheel independent suspension.
• Choice of 4 on the floor with bucket seats or steering column shift and bench seat.
• Top speed over 90 m.p.h.
DEALERS AT:
STATE WIDE DISTRIBUTORS:
R. J. GARDNER (WHOLESALE) PTY. LTD.
232 Parramatta Road, Auburn. 648-0224
Racing Car News, October, 1964, page 7
BELLETT
1600 GT

BELLETT

sports car: 'it sounds absurd to put a tiny 600 cc engine in a sports car, but this is no ordinary engine, and it does a fine job.' (See page 60 for a full track test of this car, driven by heavyweight Pete Geoghegan no less.)

Wheels magazine also produced compilations of its monthly road tests. It featured eight Japanese cars in its 1966 edition, with the Mazda 800 – 'The Mighty Atom' – considered significant enough to be on the front cover.

Another star was Nissan's Prince Skyline, in this case the GT version fitted with the two-litre engine from the Gloria, boosted by three dual-throat Weber carburettors.

These cars from Japan, have joined the world's great motoring names.

PRINCE GLORIA 6

Surprised? You won't be when you've sampled the luxury that the Prince Motor Company has built into this precision saloon. The de Dion-type rear axle is usually associated with only the most expensive high-performance British and Continental cars. And the six-cylinder engine presents you with engineering refinements you'd expect to pay quite a few hundred pounds more for.
Prince Gloria Six from: $2,678 (£1,339) incl. S/tax

PRINCE SKYLINE

Surprised? You won't be when you've tasted the swift sweet power from its one-and-a-half litre engine. Felt how sure-footedly it handles and how calmly and quietly it copes with hills. Even critical motor-writers have been impressed. And there are other advantages. Like the money you save: 18,000 miles between greasings. And refinements in engineering that you'd never expect at this price.
Skyline 1500 from only: $1,996 (£998) incl. S/tax

Prince offers a whole range of cars and commercial vehicles. And they're all proving that these engineering refinements do pay off. Proving it on roads and tracks in a lot of countries. Drive one in your locality and you'll see how.

WHEELMAR
Distributors Pty. Ltd.
(Sole distributors for N.S.W. and A.C.T.)
Olivia Lane, Surry Hills. N.S.W.
Telephone 69.7337

Wheelmar Distributors Pty. Ltd.
Olivia Lane, Surry Hills, New South Wales.
Please send me free brochure and details of the Prince Gloria ☐ Prince Skyline ☐ *(Tick Model required)*
Name
Address

It was also fitted with the four-speed Gloria gearbox. This was perhaps the first high-performance Japanese sedan to be sold here. *Wheels* put it up against the Renault Gordini, Mini Cooper 1275S and Cortina GT500 in a kind of boy racer's comparison test.

The location was the Hardie-Ferodo test track at Pitt Town outside Sydney, a high-speed oval circuit with one sharp banked corner and a larger radius flat sweeper.

'We have come up with this full comparison of the hot ones, the poor man's GTs, the four fireballs, the four cars that

must be considered by any young buck looking for a car he can hack around the street but use for trials or racing at the weekend.' Worth noting is that the Cortina GT500 was the model developed by Harry Firth especially for the 1965 Armstrong 500. The Prince Skyline GT beat Harry's hot rod and the two other contenders in top speed (111.2 mph/179 k/mh) and standing quarter-mile (17.7 seconds).

Even though a flying squad of Cooper Ss dominated the Bathurst race that year, it was the Prince that won the Pitt Town Grand Prix.

Wheels also reviewed the Datsun Cedric, the two-litre six-cylinder update of the four-cylinder Cedrics originally sold in Australia by Nissan. They had been around for five or six years, under-powered, over-priced and largely unwanted. The updated version got a more favourable review.

Over the next two or three years several more Japanese manufacturers entered the Australian market. From 1968 Subaru made a concerted effort to sell cars, initially the 1000 model, a chunky design available

Above The Subaru FF-1.
Opposite Subaru's first car.
Below The Subaru 1000.

as a two-door and four-door sedan, two-door sports coupe and four-door wagon. They featured advanced technology such as a horizontally opposed, water-cooled, four-cylinder engine made of aluminium alloy, a dual radiator cooling system and a lightweight monocoque body based on aircraft technology. The sports coupe had a high-performance engine boosted to 67 bhp by twin Hitachi carburettors, a higher compression ratio and floor shifter. Its claimed top speed was around 90 mph (145 km/h). The advanced FF-1 1100 cc version was introduced in 1969. Despite distributors in Adelaide, Brisbane and Perth, sales were not spectacular.

Isuzu's 1965 model Bellett 1500 was one of the first Japanese cars seen in Australian rally competition.

3
ROTHMANS
SOUTHERN MOUNTAINS CAR TRIAL
WHELAN MOTORS
NSW
DRO·971

Here comes the Spider

The Daihatsu Spider was the two-door convertible version of the Daihatsu Berlina saloon which had been imported back in 1965. In 1967 the Spider, with styling by Italian designer Vignale, was tested by Jim Abbott in *Auto Sportsman* magazine. 'Could this be the baby Japanese Ferrari?' he wondered. Abbott is remembered for some extremely powerful race specials – his prototype Porsche sports-racer fitted with a Shelby Cobra, for example – but he seemed genuinely impressed by the far less raunchy Daihatsu.

'It has a lot to recommend it,' he wrote. 'It is certainly a pleasant, sporty little car to drive and I feel that the Spider particularly fills the requirements of the family man with sporty aspirations.' The Daihatsu was powered by a 1000 cc four-cylinder putting out a mere 55 bhp, but this limitation was compensated by what Abbott described as 'a real honey of a gearbox ... synchromesh on all gears and the ratios are really well spaced.' He was also impressed by the electric windscreen washer, two-speed wipers and headlight dipper operated by depressing the indicator arm – all features rarely found in 1967. But testing in the middle of a Melbourne winter, he was not impressed that there was no heater, something he felt should have been included in a car with a $2000 price tag.

Melbourne agents Holstock & Jamieson had bravely offered Abbott the Spider for a week so he could have the opportunity to thrash it over some country roads near his home in Lilydale. Once out of the city, he had some reservations. 'The car steers easily at all speeds, but I did find it apt to be a little lively in the back end, particularly cornering fairly fast on a rough road, introducing axle hop which caused the back of the car to jump sideways.' He suggested a set of track rods might solve this problem.

The NAME Game

It's not easy giving a car a name. Some work instantly, like the Ford Mustang. Some don't, like the Nissan Cedric. That name was chosen by Nissan because they thought it had connotations of the English upper class. There may have been a problem in translation, but the Japanese have come up with some stinkers.

- Datsun Fairlady: it sold much better when renamed the plain old 1600.
- Datsun Sunny: the story goes that Nissan ran a national competition in Japan to name the car and received 8.5 million entries. The winning name, Sunny, was not used in Australia. The car was sold here as the Datsun 1000.

Some other questionable Japanese choices: Toyota Tiara, Hino Contessa, Daihatsu Charade, Mazda Bongo, Honda Scamp.

'See the eighth wonder of the world' was the promise for the first Australian appearance of the new Mazda Cosmo Rotary at the 1968 Sydney Royal Easter Show. Did anyone realise at the time that this space-age dream machine marked the start of more than 45 years of Mazda rotaries?

The STAR*
of the SHOW!

BATHURST 1966
the year of the Japanese

Quite a few of the Japanese cars road-tested in 1965 and 1966 were eligible for the 1966 Gallaher 500, as the annual Bathurst race for production cars was called that year. The Japanese had competed in the Great Race before but this was the year that they arrived in big numbers, and the first time they claimed a victory – not outright but in Class A. (Classes in 1966 were defined by the cars' retail prices, listed in decimal currency for the first time that year.)

Japanese cars eligible for Class A (retail value up to $1800) included the Mazda 800, in both two- and four-door formats, the Mitsubishi Colt 1000, Daihatsu Berlina, Datsun Bluebird 1300 and Toyota 700.

The Bluebird was the pre-race favourite and three were entered by the Nissan Motor Company of Australia. As expected, one driven by two factory drivers, Moto Kitano and Kunimitsi Takanashi, came first in the class. The others came second and fourth. It was a significant effort by Nissan and largely forgotten these days, even though Nissan has re-entered motorsport in Australia.

Japanese models eligible for Class B ($1801-2040) included the Mazda De Luxe, Toyota Corona 1500, Bellett 1500, Datsun Bluebird Super, Prince

Skyline 1500 (not the GT) and, yes, the Hino Contessa.

Actual entries came from Bellett (3), Toyota Corona (3) and Prince Skyline 1500 (2). But this was the year of the Mini, which comprehensively won the class, taking the first nine places outright. A Corona came fourth in the class. Despite the optional four-on-the floor gearbox, nobody was tempted to risk flying a rear-engined Hino Contessa down the mountain.

The Toyota Crown Special was eligible for Class C ($2041-2700) but so was a BMC showroom full of the all-conquering Mini Cooper S. Seventeen were entered and they dominated the race. The sole Class C Toyota Crown, driven by Bill Buckle and Alan Mottram, entered by the distributors Australian Motor Industries Ltd, finished 11th in the class. Mottie, a police pursuit driver by trade who had previously competed in ex-Victoria Police V8 Studebakers, described it as a pretty uneventful Sunday drive.

The Prince Skyline 2000 GT, which had won the *Wheels'* 'boy racer' challenge earlier that year, was eligible for the most expensive Class D ($2700-4000), as was the Datsun/Nissan Cedric De Luxe. Neither entered, probably because they would have been up

This **The Toyota Crown driven by Bill Buckle and Alan Mottram at Bathurst, 1966.**

14
C

against V8s such as the Studebaker Cruiser and Valiant Automatic.

Although Britain ruled Bathurst that day, the performance of the Japanese cars certainly impressed *Racing Car News* reporter Adrian Ryan, who walked up Mount

Panorama to watch part of the race from Shell Tower.

'On the way I had a chance to watch the cars going through XL Bend and was very impressed by the neat line of the Kitano/ Takahashi Datsun (winner of Class A). They were equally as quick as the fast Coopers through this rough corner. Up on the mountain we had a terrific view of the Reynolds/Bond clash in the Belletts (Class B). Lap after lap they were inches apart and on one memorable occasion they came into view side by side through Reid Park. Bond squeezed in front through McPhillamy's and Reynolds took him on the inside at Skyline to lead down the Esses. Great black skid marks bore testimony to some pants-wetting manoeuvres earlier in the day.'

Yes, that's the same Bond, Coli Bond, who would win the race three years later in a Holden Dealer Team Monaro. In 1966 Bond was driving a Bellett with Arthur Treloar. They finished eighth in class after losing a wheel and replacing it, according to the rules, with the spare wheel and standard jack in the boot.

If there were still some who doubted that the Japanese manufacturers were here to stay, Bathurst in 1966 would have changed their minds.

On SAFARI in New Guinea

It wasn't only the major Japanese corporations such as Nissan/Datsun and Toyota that promoted their cars in Australia, or in some cases, off shore. Isuzu, makers of the Bellett, entered production cars at Bathurst and also saw potential in rallying. This explains why Colin Bond is seen here competing in the New Guinea Safari in a car owned by the local dealership. CB could drive anything, anywhere – and win.

Bellett also imported three 'works' race cars for use by Australian drivers. These were too heavily modified to compete at Bathurst but raced at other events, driven by Pat Crea and Rod Murphy (who both ran Bellett dealerships in Melbourne) and Peter Williamson (who drove for a Sydney dealer).

DRIVER—COLLIN BOND
NAVIGATOR—BRIAN HOPE
LUCAS

NEW GUINEA MOTORS
TRAVEL
NEW GUINEA MOTORS
HARDIE-FERODO
DRIVER ÷ COLLIN BOND
NAVIGATOR ÷ BRIAN HOPE

The *Amazing* Honda S600

The Honda S600, followed by its big brother the S800, are two of the most significant Japanese cars to be released in Australia. The S600 arrived early in 1965, promoted as 'that Million-Dollar-Feeling for less than 1000 pounds'.

By now Honda was well-established as the leading manufacturer of motorcycles. It was an unknown quantity regarding automobiles.

But it had announced its intentions by building a Formula One car for the 1964 season. Designed for the existing 1.5-litre formula, the Honda F1 was certainly unusual, using a semi-monocoque chassis with the engine bolted into a rear sub-frame. The engine was a 1495 cc fuel-injected V12, producing a reported 230 bhp at 12,000 rpm. Richie Ginther won the 1965 Mexican Grand Prix in the car. In 1966 Honda built another Formula One machine for the 3-litre formula, another V12, putting out 420 bhp.

wipers, automatic windshield washers, anti-theft steering and starter motor lock — as standard equipment, not optional extras.

All this came in a small package that, as many pointed out, wasn't much bigger than your average dodgem car. Yet somehow it all worked.

Graham Howard was one of the first to test the Honda S600, soon after it was released in Australia by Bennett Honda. 'Honda's first sale problem is to show the world that this is a serious car,' he suggested, before showing his own sense of humour by convincing one of the biggest drivers to test the smallest sports car.

The Honda S600 was the first consumer car to be built by the company renowned for its technical expertise. Or 'unconventional complexity', as Graham Howard put it in the March 1965 edition of *Racing Car News*.

That was a fair description. The S600 had four synchronised carburettors — one for each cylinder — four-wheel independent suspension and double overhead camshafts, all radical technology for a road car in 1965. It also had innovations such as a wood-rimmed steering wheel, two-speed

Ian Geoghegan — or Big Pete — was best known at the time for racing Australia's most powerful Ford Mustang. 'Hey, it's all right, isn't it?' asked Pete, as he contemplated sliding in behind the wheel.

It was remarkable that he managed to fit into the car at all, but he was relatively comfortable with the top down. With Howard in the passenger seat, Pete headed down Sydney's Parramatta Road in the direction of Oran Park. Howard noted that Pete soon had the Honda up to 95 mph/153 km/h (at 9000 rpm) on the Hume Highway. That was the speedo reading. Geoghegan suggested that 85 might be a more honest estimate. Engine noise from the twin pipes was noticeable above 8500 revs. Even at that speed, there was little wind disturbance in the cockpit and cross winds had no real effect. As well, 'rough patches in the road, or uneven edges, barely disturbed the car from its line.'

Graham Howard had driven the car around town the day before and was critical of the lack of synchro on first gear, which made it difficult to engage on the move, and impossible if the speed dropped below 5 mph (8 km/h). You had to stop before finding first. He also found that the revs had to be kept up at slow speeds to avoid stalling. Both faults, he suggested, would probably be avoided with more experience behind the wheel. Engine noise would also take some getting used to. He compared the sound to a 125 cc racing two-stroke.

Out at Oran Park, Big Pete inflated the tyres to 30 lbs (13.6 kg) pressure and headed out on the circuit with Howard as a slightly nervous passenger. They did five relatively gentle laps, or so it seemed. 'However, photographer Lance Ruting informed us that the inside front wheel was about 5 inches (12.7 cm) off the ground through Energol: we found scrub marks well up the shoulder of both front tyres, and the hub-caps on the off side wheels both popped off, which suggested a bit of wheel flexing ...'

Pete wasn't even trying at that stage.

Later he did three laps on his own and went a lot harder, recording lap times of 68 seconds dead on his final two circuits.

Honda

Howard recalled Doug Chivas had recorded lap times of 67 seconds a month earlier in a Mk III Sprite, a similar car but with a modified engine nearly double the capacity.

The Honda achieved its 68-second laps with what appeared to be a minimum of fuss and, without a passenger, the front wheels remained on the ground at all times. 'His cornering method was simple,' Howard observed, 'employing a lot of revs (9000 through Energol) and twitching the car through the first part of the corner before settling down to drive smoothly out, with a change to third shortly afterwards.'

Through tighter corners Geoghegan kept the car in second throughout, powering through with controlled oversteer. 'Once a line had been started, it could be held with throttle, and the tighter or faster the corner was taken the more noise was applied. The car's behaviour is without vice, and releasing the throttle in the middle of a corner does not cause a violent twitch.'

Both Geoghegan and Howard were impressed by the tiny Honda and probably a little surprised at how good it was on the track in standard condition.

It was only a matter of time before someone developed the car into a serious racing machine. That man was Bob Riley.

The BOB RILEY Track Test

Just a few months after its launch, Bob Riley started racing a Honda S600 in production sports car events with support from distributors Bennett Honda. Even though his competition was usually much larger English sporties, from the get-go he

10

80
52
80
80

was a class winner. In 1967 Riley upgraded to the latest S800 model, which had four carburettors, 70 bhp, disc brakes and radial ply tyres. In this car he dominated the under 1100 cc sports car class.

In 1968 *Racing Car News* did a track comparison between the Riley Honda and the MG Midget driven to great success by Bob Skelton. The two were close rivals in the 'economy' class and able to beat most larger cars as well.

In some respects it was an unfair comparison, the MG having nearly twice the engine capacity of the Honda even though their external dimensions were almost identical.

At a track test on the Warwick Farm short circuit, *RCN* co-editor Rob Luck recorded nearly identical lap times although the Honda had to be thrashed – around 10,500 rpm was essential for fast laps, below 8500 you went nowhere. Luck said that it was like driving an underpowered Mini. The best time for the Midget was 44 dead compared with 44.5 for the Honda. As a comparison, Geoghegan's Mustang did 43 seconds on the short circuit.

The difference was in driving style. 'If you go into a corner too quickly in the Midget you just back off and use sideways force to slow you down and get right back on it again,' Luck said. 'Do this in the Honda and you've already spun. You tend to use more lock, or let the car run out a bit and use more road – after that you've practically run out of chances.'

These were no longer production sports cars. Both were modified for racing. The Suzuka Club in Japan had modified the Honda S800, which involved detaching the body, removing the runners and re-setting it for racing. They boosted the engine to 100 bhp from the standard 68, with fully chromed crankshaft and rods and special pistons. It was fitted with a close-ratio gearbox worth $700 in 1968 dollars, and a full pressurisation system with oil pump and filter. The suspension was completely rebuilt by the Suzuka Club. A competition clutch, which the Japanese told Riley had a maximum life of 300 miles (480 km), was fitted. After blowing a few of these, Riley replaced it with a standard clutch.

Riley's Honda was basically a Japanese works car with some personal touches. He removed the hardtop and one of the two roll-over bars. He preferred an aeroscreen to the full-size windscreen. He fitted 5½-inch (14-cm) wide wheels with Dunlop 184s and replaced the four monoblock competition carbs supplied by the factory with twin dual throat Webers.

Bob Riley maintained the car himself. What a pocket rocket it proved to be. In 1968, when the car was tested, it had yet to be beaten in its under-1100 cc class. The Honda won outright at Catalina Park at its first meeting, then took lap records for its class at Amaroo and Warwick Farm, and broke the outright production sports car record at Mallala previously held by Bob Jane's lightweight E-type.

Honda

The ANNE WILLS Honda

It really helped to be an extrovert if you wanted to drive a Honda sports — you couldn't help but be noticed. Anne Wills, a popular Adelaide TV presenter, obviously liked to be noticed. Her brand-new Honda was featured in *People* magazine. She chose one in bright yellow: 'Perhaps a little ostentatious?' she asked *People* — with tongue in her cheek of course.

Dave Dunsmore's S600

The new Honda S600 also had surprising success in another branch of motorsport. Driving Tests – also known as Motorkhanas, or Parking Lot GPs – were a popular club activity in the late 1960s, with major events covered in magazines like *Racing Car News*. Acceleration and manoeuvrability were the keys, plus a high degree of driving skill.

In 1967 Dave Dunsmore entered his standard road-registered Honda, complete with luggage rack, in some rounds of the New South Wales championship. He was up against the traditional modified Minis and Sprites, plus serious stuff such as Warren Tite's Tahmoor Special, one of the first machines to be built especially for the sport. The Newcastle round of the state title was held on a gravel surface at the Metro Drive-In complex. Dunsmore recorded fastest time of the day for the Square Flag Bend and then won the round with fastest time in the Cloverleaf test.

EAW·495
13

Honda

Thrashing the Scamp

Launched in October 1968, Honda's front-wheel-drive, overhead camshaft, four-stroke Scamp was initially promoted as a family runabout: 'luxury comfort for four adults — with room for two sets of golf clubs in the boot.' It sold for the bargain price of $1397.

Mr and Mrs Everage were not yet convinced that Japanese cars were as good as the equivalents made in Britain or Australia. So New South Wales distributors Bennett Honda devised a clever publicity stunt to show just how reliable these tiny machines could be. They announced that two brand-new Scamps would attempt a seven-day, seven-night marathon, which was non-stop except for fuel and driver changes. This endurance event would take place in and around the centre of Sydney and would include morning and afternoon peak periods. The route also involved a drive through the heart of Kings Cross, which must have been an interesting experience at 3AM.

Two demonstrator cars were chosen at random by *Modern Motor* magazine staff at the Bennett Honda dealership in William Street. Both had 21 miles (34 km) on the clock when the marathon began.

The nearby Top of the Cross Golden Fleece service station was specified as the only location where drivers could make a pit stop and where driver changes were made every five hours. Whenever the cars were filled up with fuel, *Modern Motor* staffers supervised the sealing of the fuel tanks and oil filters.

To boost publicity, both Scamps had large scoreboards fixed to the rear of the car recording mileage, miles per gallon and hours run. These were updated daily in chalk. This allowed drivers stuck behind them to follow the daily progress of the two cars.

The results were impressive. At the end of the 168 hours, both Scamps recorded average fuel consumption of 54.5 miles per gallon, despite driving through peak-hour traffic. The average speed worked out to just under 30 mph (48 km). At the finish, one Scamp had travelled a distance of 4955.8 miles (7975.5 km) with a total fuel bill of $37.74. The second achieved 4968 miles (7995.2 km) with costs of $37.43.

The only mechanical repairs required were minor clutch adjustments on both cars. And one Scamp needed an oil top up, the other didn't.

'Bennett Honda have proved their point we think – that the Scamp is an economical, reliable form of basic transport,' concluded *Modern Motor.* 'On that basis we are happy to commend it to readers.'

The team at *Racing Car News* magazine also tested Honda's mini machine in June 1968, beginning their story with 'You may well ask, what the hell is a Honda Scamp doing in *RCN*?'

Their answer was that when they read through the car's specs they had thought about its potential for Sports/Racing (Closed) – better known as Sports Sedans. They were impressed by its low weight – at 1047 lbs (475 kg), it was more than 300 lbs lighter than a Mini Deluxe – and suggested that one fitted with a larger, developed motor could well challenge all those lightweight Minis dominating the category.

To prove the point, *RCN* editors Max Stahl and Rob Luck showed how easy it was to lift a standard Scamp off the ground. They also demonstrated that, when driven hard, a Scamp would lift a rear wheel in the same manner as a Mini racer.

Plans to turn one into a race contender never quite eventuated, although a few appeared in Class A, the cheapest category in Series Production racing. Two were used to set endurance records.

In September 1970, a Scamp N350, the bargain-basement version, was driven by Heather Brock and publicist Pam Elam to set several endurance records at Sandown Park. Doug Hicks and Ron McCormack drove the larger N600 over the same circuit. The pair of cars set a total of 18 Australian records over six hours at average speeds of around 60 mph (96.5 km/h).

Given the scarcity of other cars that small, these records may well still exist.

The average man and woman on the street were also impressed by Honda's new Scamp. It enjoyed considerable sales success – more as a no-frills city commuter than as a family runabout.

And the Scamp was especially popular among a new generation of independent young women.

Honda's 1300 *Coupe*

One of Honda's first serious 'normal' sized sports cars was the 1300 Coupe – the last car personally overseen by Honda founder Soichiro Honda.

Honda said of the new car when it was launched at the 1968 Tokyo Motor Show: 'The basic management philosophy of our company is originality, and accordingly our goal has always been to spur demand by introducing products that only Honda can create.'

They weren't kidding – the thing handled

like a racing car. Honda had managed to extract 100 bhp (75 kW) from the little 1300 cc four.

This salient point was not lost on the Toyota Industries president Eiji Toyoda, who was observed spending a good ten minutes at the Motor Show checking out the new Honda before calling over his engineers for a quick cha.

If Honda had get 100 horsepower from a 1300cc engine, he asked them, then why can't we?

Bonsai 800

The Toyota Sports 800, introduced in 1965, bore a resemblance to the later 2000 but was powered by a smaller 79 cc horizontally opposed twin-cylinder motor developing 70 bhp at 7750 rpm, with a top speed of 97 mph (156 km/h). An obvious competitor to Honda's S600 and S800 sports cars, it was slightly larger and somewhat cheaper. It was closer in size to a Triumph Spitfire. The Honda was more sophisticated technically, but the Sports 800 had its design innovations: synchromesh on all four gears, two-speed wipers, an adjustable grille vent and a locking fuel cap. A petrol-powered heater which had a tendency to explode was an option best avoided. Around 300 were built up till 1969.

S 800

Toyota 2000 GT

Often described as the Japanese E Type, the Toyota 2000 GT was made in relatively small numbers from 1967 to 1970.

Most reports say that only 351 were built, including a small number of race and movie cars. For a car that is so desirable today, it was strangely unpopular at the time. Around 150 were exported, with only a handful — perhaps as few as three — coming to Australia. It was once thought that very few survived but over a hundred are now recorded around the world. One that is in very good condition is now worth around $350,000 in US dollars.

The 2000 GT was a beautiful design at a time when Japanese cars were noted for their practicality but not for their looks. The Toyota Company obviously recognised its good looks: at its Kuragake Commemorative Hall, one was displayed pointing skywards

as if about to be launched into space. The car design incorporated typical Japanese eccentricities, such as the series of hatches carved into the body to allow access to the battery, radiator and brake fluid.

The pop-up headlights, though, were possibly a last-minute consideration to meet the US regulation that specified that lights had to be at least 24 inches (61 cm) off the ground.

The car featured a liquid-cooled, four-stroke, six-cylinder, 12-valve DOHC motor, with a capacity of 1.98 litres. Toyota had originally planned to install a small V8 but instead adapted the SOHC M-Type Crown six-cylinder motor, converting it to DOHC specifications. It was a tight fit, requiring the air filter to be relocated. Included was a five-speed manual and all-synchromesh gearbox. An oil cooler was fitted as standard.

Power was rated as 150 bhp at 7000 rpm. Top speed was 220 km/h. It excelerated from 0 to 60 mph (96.6 km/h) in 8.4 seconds, covering the standing quarter in 15.9 seconds, roughly 2 seconds faster than the Datsun 260Z could claim in 1974.

The 2000 GT motors were developed in conjunction with Yamaha, which made the cylinder heads, among other goodies (the engine compartment was fitted with a badge stating that it was built by Yamaha for Toyota). The car was launched at the 1965 Tokyo Motor Show and promoted in October 1966 with a

78-hour continuous endurance run at the Yatanabe Test Track, during which three world and 13 international records were broken. Average speeds of over 200 km/h were set on the banked track. The yellow and green car featured in photographs – thought to be the prototype – was one of four development mules used on that occasion. Innovations for the record attempt included a Perspex bug deflector on the bonnet. Holes were cut in the bonnet so that fluids could be poured in without opening it up during pit stops. Four drivers rotated during the endurance run.

The two most famous Toyota 2000s are those built for the 1967 James Bond movie *You Only Live Twice*. They were white convertibles, especially created for the film by Toyota because the 6 foot 3 inch (189-cm) Sean Connery complained that he couldn't fit into the coupe.

The sequences were filmed at the Pinewood Studios in London with the actors in a stationary car in front of moving background footage. These scenes were interspersed with footage of a second car, driven by Toyota test drivers through the streets of Tokyo.

A range of 007 gadgets were fitted into the car's rear compartment. Most were

supplied by Sony and included a tiny closed-circuit TV with VCR unit in the glove-box, a two-way radio, voice-controlled tape recorder and a hi-fi receiver.

Despite its efforts in producing the two convertibles, Toyota was disappointed when only six minutes of footage of the car appeared in the final cut.

Lately the 007 Toyota has emerged as a major movie celebrity, usually nominated as one of the top three Bond cars in surveys. In 1977 one of the cars used in *You Only Live Twice* was located in Hawaii

TOYOTA 2000GT
Esso
TOYOTA
2000GT

and bought by the manufacturer. It is now in the Toyota museum in Tokyo.

Fifty-four 2000 GTs were exported to America in 1967 but the response was sluggish and the model was soon dropped, perhaps because its US price of $7500 was more than a Jaguar E Type. Only one car is thought to have been imported to Britain, and that ended up being owned by model-of-the-moment Twiggy.

In Australia one was on show at Bill Buckle's Toyota dealership in Brookvale when Buckle wasn't using the car as his personal vehicle.

Another went on display at Jim Abbott's International Racing and Sports Car Show at the Melbourne Exhibition Building in early 1969, before being toured to other state capitals. The 2000 GT was on the Brent's Sports Cars stand, parked alongside a Ford Cobra.

It had plenty of competition elsewhere. Other cars at the show included an STP Turbine Indy car, a Mercedes 300SLR, an Alfa Tipo 33, the Frank Matich SR4 sports-racer and – possibly the star of the show – the new Ford V8-powered Bolwell Nagari. It was noted that the Bolwell brothers were taking orders as fast as they could. Sales of the Toyota were far less spectacular.

Classic DATSUN

When the Datsun 1600 was launched in Sydney in early 1968, most new cars were still fitted with cross-ply tyres as standard. In fact, George Denner, general manager of Nissan Australia, commented at the launch that 'radial ply tyres are just a sales gimmick to fool the public'. What he meant by that bold statement was that radials were only suited to a minority of drivers for certain cars. The majority, in his opinion, could survive quite well on old technology rubber.

This was the basis of some debate at the time, and the team from *Racing Car News* decided to replace the Dunsafe cross-plies fitted to their test Datsun because they had the feeling that the new radials would be safer at speed. They fitted a set of Veith radials, pumped up to 28 psi, for a planned trip to Surfers and back.

Surprisingly, the standard Datsun wasn't fitted with seat belts either, something that prompted the test team to consider cancelling the test. But they drove on regardless.

Testing cars for magazines was a lot of fun back then. The *RCN* team drove the Datto to Surfers and back for the 1968 Tasman race meeting on 9 February. When the constant rain permitted, this included some periods of 90 mph (145 km/h) touring on the Pacific Highway. This was achieved with at least one passenger asleep in the back seat, another dozing in the front passenger seat. The driver appears to have stayed awake.

This was a test of a brand-new car — which

ETU-313
DATSUN
VIC
KVD·597

turned out to be one of Nissan's most successful ever – but also a test of new tyre technology. Despite George Denner's opinion, the *RCN* verdict was that radials felt a lot safer on wet roads. 'Significantly, the tyres never once let go in a corner ... despite a feeling of aquaplaning when large pools of water were hit, the steering never lost its feel or control.'

Initial impressions were that the new Datsun was a joy to drive at speed on the open highway, although it was obvious that a certain amount of smoothness had been sacrificed to improve handling. 'This apparently was achieved in the conventional Japanese fashion – slightly too harsh spring rates and correspondingly soft damper rates.' This made the car a little skittish when driven hard on a bumpy or uneven surface. *RCN*'s advice was to simply slow down when this started to happen.

Some minor complaints. The Datsun 1600's windscreen had been poorly fitted and leaked, and the interior tended to mist up, requiring regular cleaning of the windows with tissues. The deluxe version had a heater/demister, plus booster fans, but the standard test vehicle had only dashboard vents. The windows couldn't be opened

because of torrential rain. And the two-speed windscreen wipers tended to lift off the glass at over 50 mph (80 km/h).

The test included a session on the Surfers Paradise circuit. The most interesting observation was recorded during some laps in pouring rain. 'After setting the car with a fixed amount of lock for the second half of the left-hander in the Esses, it was possible to pound the car through flat throttle until it oversteered itself into an angle of some 60 or 70 degrees with the roadway without correction. The car could then be held in this position simply with throttle adjustment, but no steering alteration until the right hander was approached ...'

Lap times in the dry, on road radials, compared favourably with those of an 1100 cc Mini Cooper S in Series Production mode. Using the current class system used for Bathurst racing (based on showroom retail price rather than capacity), the cheapest Cooper S would have been a direct competitor but probably would have beaten the Datsun 1600 anyway.

The *RCN* team decided that the new Datsun had more potential for Improved Production racing, based on one already raced by Barry Tapsall. 'The 1600 SSS should be very interesting,' they predicted.

12

BIG NEWS! U.S. 200 MPH DRAG TEAM COMING!
wheels
AUSTRALIA'S TOP MOTORING MAGAZINE
MARCH, 1966
Registered at the G.P.O., Sydney, for transmission by post as a periodical.
30c.
3/-
SHOCK FACTS ON DEALER SERVICE!
A·0759
WE DRIVE SLASHING NEW CORONA HARDTOP
• DRIVING BMC's GLAMOR PRINCESS
• SEAT BELTS: THE COST FACTOR
• FULL-SCALE TEST OF FAMILY CARAVAN

While Toyota was committed to mass-producing cars that appealed to the average punter, the company occasionally surprised with something out of the ordinary. Which explains why a new Corona Hardtop, the 1600-S, was significant enough to appear on the cover of *Wheels* in March 1966.

'Swinging styling in a two-door Japanese hardtop' ran the headline inside the magazine, after the car was given a brief road test on trade plates in Sydney. 'Fully imported, and expensive at nearly $3000 the Corona

The Corona GT

1600-S is less a rich man's plaything than a hard-going, fine-handling individual's car,' was the conclusion.

The main improvement noted over the standard four-door sedan was a twin-carburettor 1587 cc engine, giving out 95 bhp compared with the standard 74 bhp. Japanese figures claimed an optimistic standing quarter in 17.7 seconds. Disc brakes were fitted to the front, the first Corona sold in Australia given this feature.

The car was first shown at the Sydney Motor Show in late 1965, and its sleek exterior design attracted large numbers of admirers. This car, red with black trim, was the same one tested by *Wheels.* At the time, it was the only one in the country and, although allegedly there was a long list of orders taken, these cars remain ultra rare.

In 1968, another interpretation on the hardtop theme was the Corona 1600 GT. The two-door coupe design transformed Toyota's basic family sedan into something out of an Italian movie. And they backed it up with some goodies inspired by the 2000 GT sports car.

Yamaha developed the twin-cam head for the 2000 GT project and they also designed one for the Corona GT. This gave the humble Corona close to 110 bhp, which fully kicked in at 6500 rpm. A five-speed gearbox was an option, just in case you wanted to use all that power. This made it a challenge to drive around town, but a joy on the highway.

'Suspension-wise the car is designed for the enthusiast,' suggested *Racing Car News,* which previewed the first Corona GT as supplied to Buckle Toyota. 'The Japanese method of obtaining instant good handling is to firm up everything – springs, dampers, the lot – which is fine for smooth surfaces and moderate-to-high speeds, but not so hot elsewhere.' But it was pointed out that a genuine enthusiast would put up with the occasional rough ride on rough surfaces.

The Corona GT featured independent front suspension and wide-blade rear semi-elliptics with twin torque rods on the rear.

The 10.6 inch (26.9 cm) discs on the front, boosted by servos, made sure the thing stopped. Drums were fitted to the rear, also servo assisted.

The biggest surprise for the average Corona owner was inside the car, where the same bucket seats fitted to the 2000 GT were featured in an all-black decor. Safety belts were fitted as standard (although they were not yet compulsory in Australia), as were full carpeting, a push-button radio, power antenna, a heater/demister, electric screen washers and, considered a luxury at the time, a dashboard clock.

The Corona GT was imported and for sale from Buckle Toyota and selected dealers, on an 'order and wait' basis. Price in Aussie dollars was around the $4400 mark, at a time when the base-model Corona, built in Australia, cost less than $2000.

The GT featured in *RCN* bore the distinctive BB-818 numberplate, suggesting it was driven by Bill Buckle himself. And yes, those were wire wheels fitted to the boss's car. These aren't mentioned in the *Wheels*' story but certainly don't look out of place.

Buckle had a habit of importing Japanese rarities and, when he wasn't driving them around Sydney's Northern Beaches, he would display the cars prominently in his Brookvale showroom. As well as the GT, he also did this with a Toyota 2000 GT. He knew that passing motorists would stop and pop in for a look, and if they couldn't afford the luxury import, they'd probably be interested in one of the basic models.

In 1969 came the Corona Mark II 1900 SL, 6 inches (15 cm) longer than the existing Corona sedan, placing it in between the Crown and the Corolla. Of the Mark II range, only the two-door hardtop would be available in Australia, Peter Robinson reported in *Australian Motor Sports*.

At $3695 (manual) or $3795 (automatic), sales of the Mark II were expected to be limited. Those prices put it up against imports like the Fiat 124 coupe.

Performance figures were impressive though. The larger single overhead camshaft engine gave the Mark II a claimed top speed of 110 mph (177 km/h). 'It should find a small but steady group of buyers,' predicted Robbo. But again, actual sales were sluggish. (If you can find one for sale today, expect to pay big money for it.)

Tokyo Motor Show

The 1967 Tokyo Motor Show – the 14th held since 1954 – attracted over 1.4 million visitors. This was the first sighting of the Nissan Bluebird 510, as well as Toyota's flagship V8 model, the Century which was sold mainly in Japan.

SUZUKI
SPORTS CORNER
SUZUKI FRONTE 800
出口
10

コルト1500
スポーツセダン
MAZDA RX 87

The CB Colt

While some manufacturers put all their promotional eggs in the Bathurst basket, Mitsubishi realised that their Colt series of cars had more chance of success in rallying. Fortunately, this sport was at its peak in the late 1960s, with major events such as the Southern Cross International Rally attracting as much media attention as the Mount Panorama enduro.

Mitsubishi's master stroke was in the driver selection.

Mitsubishi Australia decided that a smart young guy called Colin Bond had some star potential. Bond's talented navigator Brian Hope also deserves some credit for their combined success.

In 1967 and 1968, before he was 'discovered' by Harry Firth and the Holden Dealer Team, CB turned the tiny Colt Fastback into a giant killer. One of the team's first successes was at the 1967 Southern Cross International, then sponsored by

Rothmans, where Colts finished first and third in Class F, second in Class A and second in Class E.

Bond finished fourth outright, raising a few eyebrows along the way, although an even more impressive performance was by team-mate Doug Stewart, who managed to attract attention in the biggest possible way. 'As Stewart glanced down at this safety belt coupling, a "dip" sign flashed past at almost 100 mph [161 km/h] and next thing the Colt hit. The first leap carried 17 yards [15.5 m], the second (including an end-for-end somersault) 83 yards [76 m], and three tyres burst on the impact. Slewing off the road, the car hurdled an embankment, hit once more, then Stewart lost it and the car crashed into a fence. Howzat!' (A yard is a little less than a metre.)

This dramatic eyewitness account was recorded by navigator John Bryson, who was sitting in the passenger seat as it happened.

EPM 387

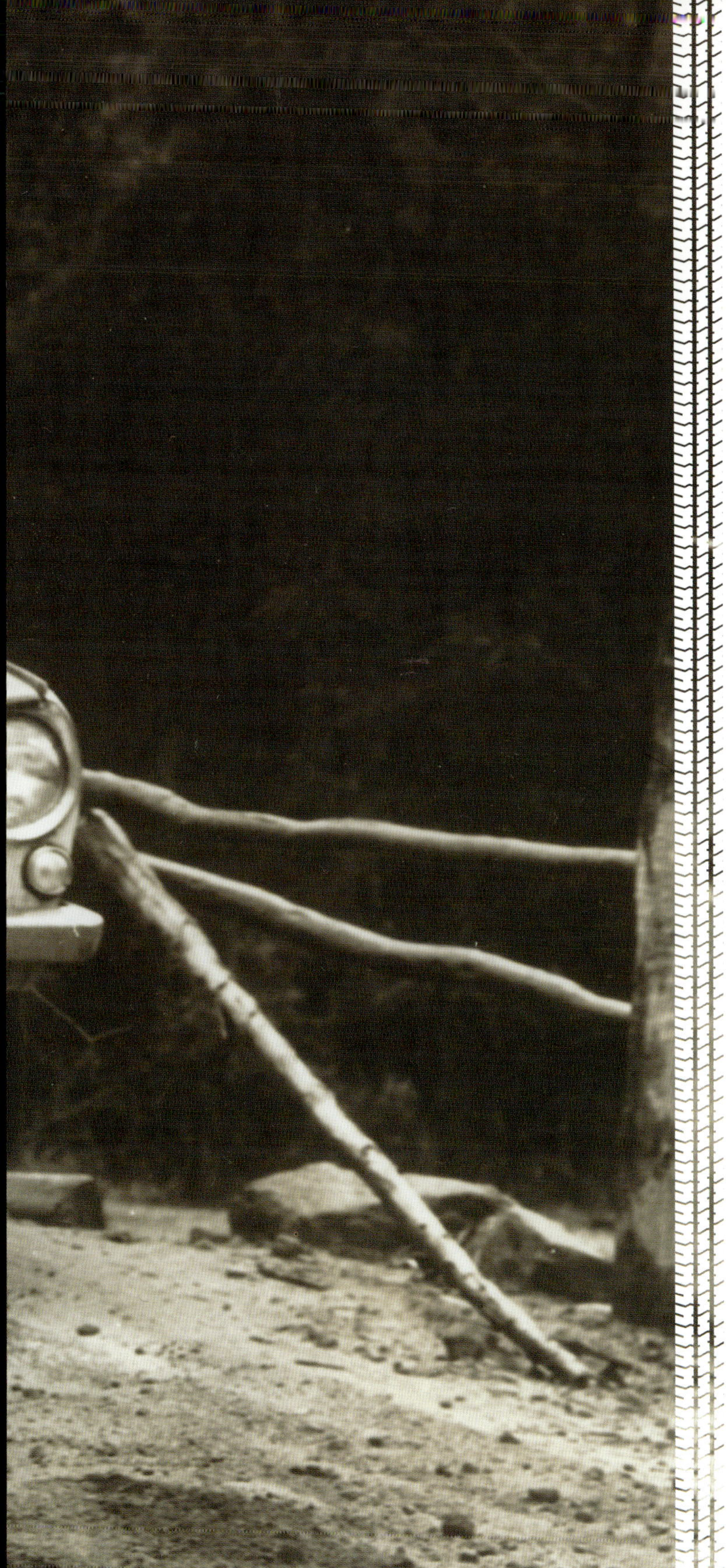

He must have paced out the distances between impacts while waiting for the service crew to arrive. Miraculously, they managed to get the Colt back on the road and Stewart finished the event. This was the car that ran third in Class F.

Colin Bond's result was considered so extraordinary that his car, still in Southern Cross livery and coated with some prime Australian dirt, was prominently displayed at the 1967 Tokyo Motor Show.

In the 1968 Southern Cross, Bond stepped it up a notch and finished an astonishing third overall, with another Colt in ninth place. These two cars finished first and second in Class G. As an indication of how good Bond was, he recorded the fastest time on the special stage around the Hume Weir race circuit, and also won the stage around the Bilpin scrambles (motorcross) track.

The Bond-Hope combo scored an outright victory that year in state-level competition, winning the KLG 300 in July. In the process, they beat all the top New South Wales competitors, including Evan Green in a Mini-Cooper S entered by BMC Australia.

This inspired Rob Luck, co-editor of *Racing Car News*, to conduct an extensive test drive of the Colin Bond rally special, which he took on with some scepticism.

'Until a few weeks ago,' Luck wrote, 'I thought a Colt Fastback was a misshapen, spunkless, uninspiring Japanese automotive industry joke.'

The one Luck was given to test was the actual Colin Bond factory special. This was the prototype for the Colt rally specials of the future: 'the product of two years of intensive development Mitsubishi Australia has planned-out with the cars in Australia. The rally field has served as proving ground, test market and product planning and development media, and it has been responsible for constant improvement and rebuilding of the cars.'

Luck was quickly forced to eat his introductory words. This Colt had plenty of spunk. In its 1968 specs, the works Colt was now putting out 76 bhp from its basic 1100 cc motor, thanks to multiple carburettors, modified manifolds and a hot camshaft. This made it capable of speeds over 100 mph (161 km/h), although 95 was the highest recorded by Luck. The car did the standing quarter in the low- to mid-18 seconds bracket and 0 to 60 mph in 11.4 seconds. As comparison, the standard Colt did 0 to 60 in 19.6 seconds.

Other improvements from standard included all gearbox and final drive ratios

Right The Colin Bond car at the Tokyo Motor Show attracting attention.

reversed, tandem master cylinders, front discs instead of drums and high-pressure oil pump, plus the full range of rally options, including a bigger fuel tank. These bits were supplied ex-factory. In Japan, a rally package was available for most sedans.

It was on the dirt, with CB driving and Luck sweating in the navigator's seat, that this pocket rocket really performed, with Bond thrashing it around a well-known stretch of road alongside the Colo River near Windsor. Luck was as impressed by Colin Bond, still a relatively unknown talent, as he was by the obviously potent weapon he was riding in.

He noted, as Harry Firth also did, that the young man always drove within his own limits according to the conditions, unlike some other top drivers who were clearly over the edge. The edge, in this case, was a 100-foot (30-m) sheer drop to the Colo River.

Rob Luck was also impressed that Mitsubishi Australia had decided to release a limited-edition rally production car in early 1969. These specials were slightly less wild than Bond's car, but they still had the 76 bhp engine, front and rear disc brakes, twin Solex carbs, special exhaust manifold and 'a few fiddles in the valve department'. The expected price was around the $2200 range, $250 more than the standard two-door Colt.

Luck noted that the full-bore works car was still suitable for road use, as it had to be. In 1968 all Australian rally cars were road-registered and driven from stage to stage. No million-dollar transporters allowed.

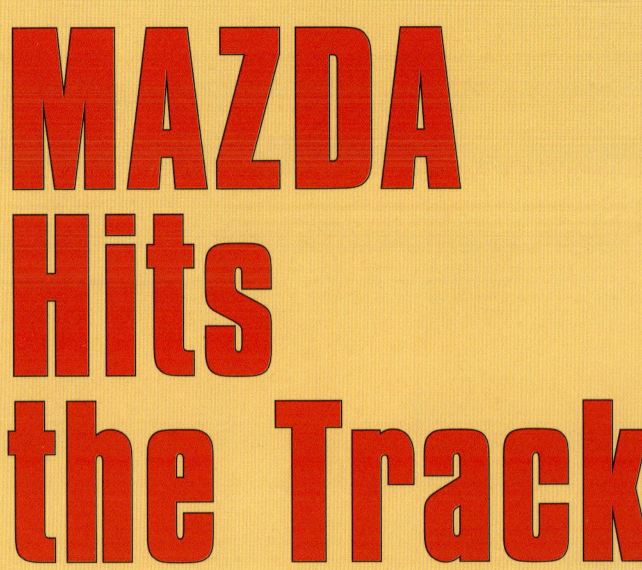

MAZDA Hits the Track

Following the success of the 1500, Mazda introduced its new contender in the small car class early in 1969. This was a competitive market. At the time, this low-budget category was dominated by the Mini, Datsun 1000 and Toyota Corolla.

XL"
ASTR
BE
DHW-007

Mazda offered two versions: the basic four-door sedan and a two-door coupe with a more sporty appearance.

Both had a 1169 cc four-in-line OHV motor, giving out a claimed 73 bhp at 6000 rpm. The main mechanical difference was in gearing and brakes. The sedan had lower ratios in first and second gears, which made it nippier in city driving. The coupe had a higher third gear,and was fitted with front disc brakes, the first in its category to have these fitted as standard. The sedan had the regulation four drums.

The two-door coupe was 2 inches (5 cm) lower in overall height despite being fitted with larger 13-inch (33-cm) wheels (the sedan's were 12-inch (30.5 cm) wheels. The coupe's lap-sash seatbelts fitted as standard, plus tacho and tripmeter were options for the sedan.

The Mazda 1200 was an interesting design, not unlike a condensed 1500, but most critics thought it sat a little too high off the ground. And not everyone preferred the two-door model. 'The sedan is, strangely, the better looker,' wrote Peter Wherrett in his test for *Racing Car News* magazine in March 1969. He compared the two versions on the road, noting that the four-door had better initial acceleration thanks to its lower gearing. When he took the two-door to Oran Park he soon realised its greater potential, especially when he pushed it a little. 'We made all changes at 6000 [rpm] but from previous experience with the willing little Japanese engines, 6500 seems reasonable and with an engine which has been balanced and well-prepared, 7000 should be safe when it was needed ...'

Wherrett only had a brief session that day but found that the higher third gear was good for over 90 mph (145 km/h), then calculated that 110 mph (177 km/h) plus was possible if you revved it to 7000 in fourth. 'You'll probably never see it, but it's there theoretically.' He didn't test this out because the demonstrator car he was driving hadn't been fully run in and was fitted with road tyres that hadn't been inflated to the preferred race pressures.

His main complaints were the artificial wood-grain steering wheel and a slippery gear knob. Overall, the Mazda handled pretty well, despite a tendency to lift a front wheel when cornered hard. 'Imagine this car fully tweaked, lowered, with 5 inch [12.5 cm] rims and racing tyres,' he said.

As it turned out, both these cars would be eclipsed as race-track performers by

the amazing Mazda R100 rotary. It first appeared at Bathurst in 1969 where Gary Cooke and Geoff Spence steered it to an impressive 19th outright. Trevor and Neil Mason finished 21st in another R100. The car competed in Class C, for those with a retail price of $2251 to $3100, which put them up against the Fiat 125, Ford Capri 1600, Mini Cooper S and, of all things, the Valiant Pacer. Even so, it was competitive.

An even more spectacular result was achieved in that 1969 race by Bernie Haehnle, the Formula Vee champion who was driving a third Mazda rotary that had been entered by Dennis Whitehead of Denlo Motors. Whitehead invited Wherrett to co-

KL"
ASTR
BE
DHW 007

LEFT & ABOVE Bernie Haehnle's superhuman efforts to right his car is one of the most memorable moments in Bathurst history.

drive the car. Wherrett accepted the offer but he knew from experience that driving one around Mount Panorama would be a challenge, given that these cars were running to Series Production specs on skinny road tyres.

'Bernie took the first practice session and when he came in he told me, in his strong German accent, that it was "a bit hairy",' wrote Wherrett in his autobiography. 'He was putting it mildly. The car had been constructed on a narrow track and the track-to-wheelbase ratio was all wrong: that is to say, it was either too long or too narrow, one or the other.'

The result was a tendency to oversteer without warning, not a pleasant experience coming flat out through the dipper and down the mountain. Nevertheless, the radical rotary engine had plenty of speed and the fearless Haehnle qualified near the top of his category.

Haehnle was used to driving at absolutely ten-tenths in his Vee and that was how he started in the R100. Around lap 30, Wherrett and the pit crew noticed that he didn't come past when he should have. They soon realised why. The television coverage showed the little white Mazda off the road and upside down in the grass near the top of the mountain.

Bernie Haehnle crawled out of the car and decided that he wanted to continue in the race. He grabbed a fence post and used it as a lever to try and tip the car back on to four wheels. According to the rules, he had to do this without any outside assistance. The flaggies can be seen watching in stunned amazement.

This feat of strength took him over an hour, with the other cars flying past at full speed just a few metres away. When Haehnle finally managed to flip the car over, he jumped in, started it up and returned down the hill to the pits.

Right The stylish Mazda 1500 looked more like an Italian car, which is not surprising given the shape was designed by Italian stylist Giorgetto Giugiaro.

Unfortunately, the front windscreen had smashed in the incident so the officials wouldn't allow him to continue in the race, despite Haehnle's suggestion that he remove the rear windscreen as well and continue the drive with goggles on.

Haehnle's superhuman efforts gained him a lot more television exposure than if the team had completed the race in traditional fashion.

'Not surprisingly, Dennis Whitehead was delighted,' noted Wherrett, who wasn't quite so happy. He didn't get to drive one lap in the race.

SS
A 1500

The *demon* Datsun

'How come there are so few Datsuns around when they can be made to go like this?' was the big question asked by *Racing Car News* track tester Peter Wherrett.

In December 1969 he reviewed the Datsun SR311 sports car – better known as the Datsun 2000 – which David Mingay and Richard Carter had developed into a very effective sports-racer, competing in the production sports category. It was an obvious choice for racing yet Mingay and Carter were two of only a few to see its raw potential.

The 2000 was a vast improvement on the 1600 Datsun sports cars. Those extra 40 cc took it to a new level. 'The single overhead cam engine is a high performance engine in the truest form,' Wherrett noted. 'Very little is needed to modify the factory engine into a reliable competition engine. The bottom end is strong enough to withstand any additional strain that may be placed upon it. The bearing surfaces are sufficiently large to accept the loads of racing competition. The crank and rods are beautifully engineered and present no problems used as they come with the car.'

The five-speed gearbox was also ideal for racing purposes. Wherrett was a fan, describing the Datsun 2000 as the best road sports car value in Australia.

David Mingay initially bought the car as his daily drive in 1968 but, as a race enthusiast, soon took it out to Warwick Farm for some club racing. He fitted wider wheels and had a head job done but otherwise it was standard and road-registered. He scored a win and a second place at his first meeting.

He then fitted a set of R7 Dunlops – the beginning of a systematic transformation into a race machine. He teamed up with his friend Richard Carter, already racing an outdated MGA, which he decided to sell and share the driving of the Datsun.

They fitted a factory 4.5 rear end, a front sway bar, lowered the car by an inch and added twin 45 mm Webers. A Seton extractor was fitted for the car's first open class meeting at Bathurst and the cam was reground. The car blew a clutch in practice, but before this setback they recorded a top speed of 131 mph (211 km/h) down Con Rod.

At this stage, the motor was putting out 170 bhp at 7000 rpm. Compression ratio was 12:1.

For the 1969 Catalina meeting, the guards were extended to allow a set of Firestone Indy race tyres mounted on 8-inch (20-cm) rims to be fitted. The windscreen was replaced by a Perspex race screen.

With Richard Carter driving, the Datsun finished third, just behind Ross Bond's more powerful Austin-Healey 3000. Ross Bond was then the king of the production sports category, but the Datsun recorded the fastest lap of the race. Suddenly the pair were in the big league.

By now Mingay and Carter were experimenting with a front spoiler which, along with the extended wheel arches, made the car look more modified than it really was. Underneath, things were still pretty similar to a Datsun sold in the showroom, including the original rear drum brakes. Servo-assisted discs were only on the front wheels.

Mingay and Carter told Wherrett that they still had around two years' worth of developments to go, with future plans including fully rose-jointed suspension, a rear sway bar, further engine development and a close ratio gearbox.

In the state the car was in, Wherrett was blown away by its performance on the Oran Park circuit. Power could be applied anywhere from 4000 rpm to the recommended 6500 limit, with enough grunt to exit corners on controlled oversteer.

'It is the most "moreish" car I have driven this year,' Wherrett wrote after his brief test session. 'Thoroughly delightful, fast, safe and bags of fun.'

His best lap of the circuit was 53 seconds. Mingay and Carter had got down to 52 seconds and with further improvements were aiming at breaking the 50-second barrier.

The Datsun 2000 proved to be a particularly good training ground for Richard Carter. By 1976 he had switched to a

Formula Ford and that year he won the TAA Driver to Europe championship series. First prize was a trip to England to further his professional career.

The Hot Zot

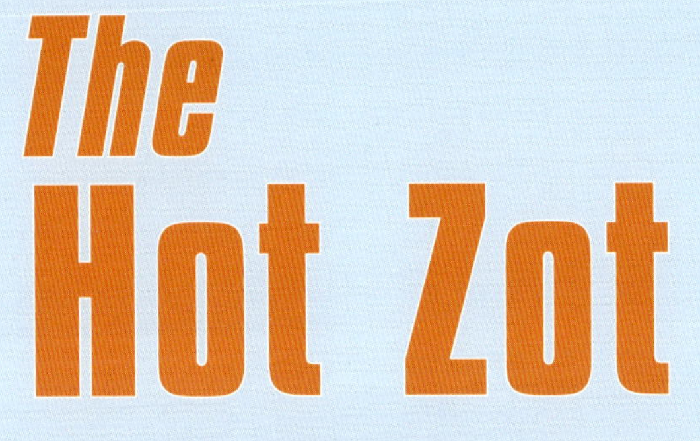

Nobody, it seems, took the Honda Z too seriously. 'It really is a cute toy of a motor car which is handy for certain uses and useless for others,' suggested Ray Bell in the November 1972 edition of *Racing Car News*. 'Tiny it is, well equipped it also is and the performance, well ...' He might have been joking when he claimed that, with some patience, the Z might even go fast enough to break some speed limits.

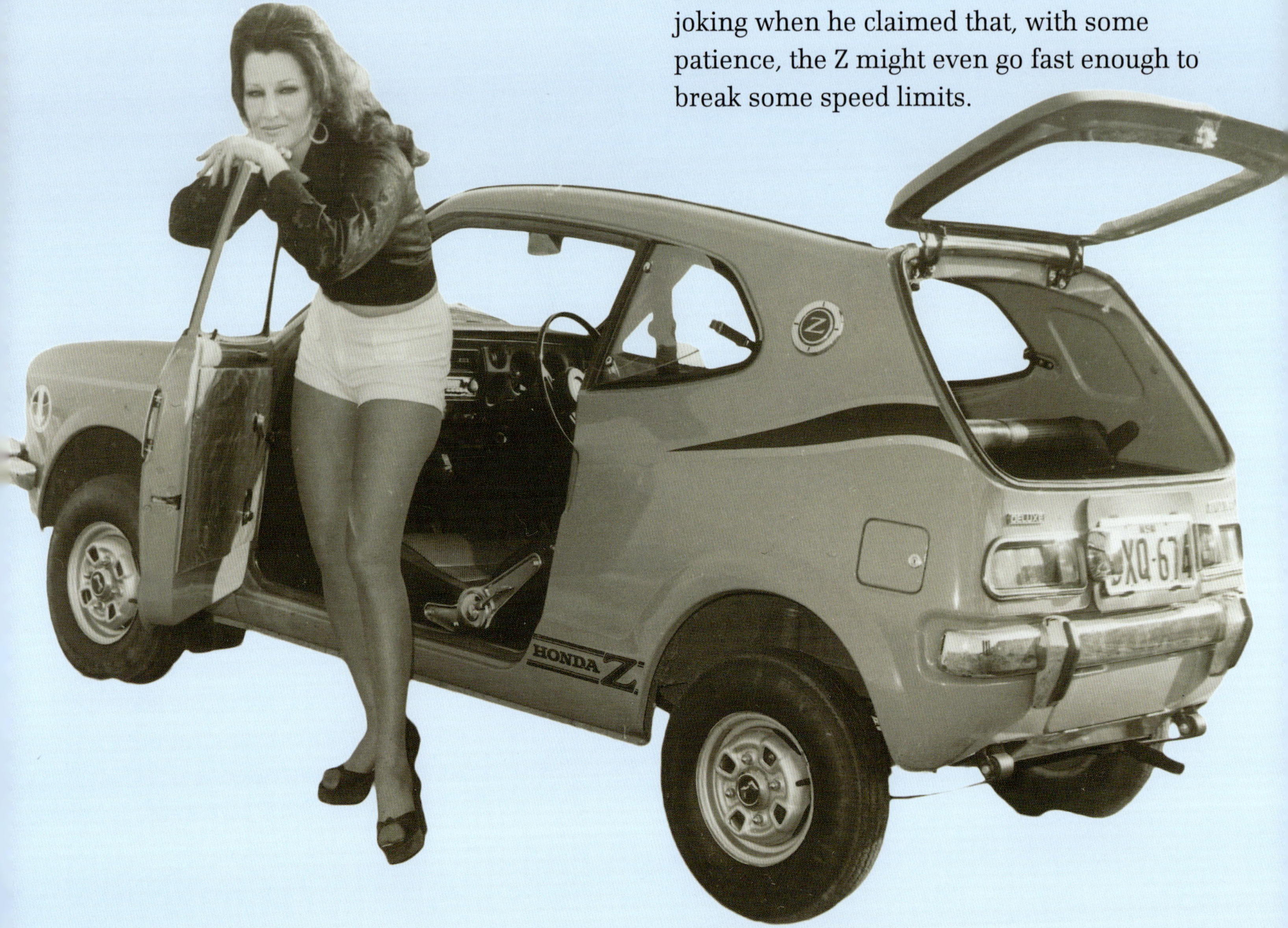

Mechanically, the car was based on the successful Honda Scamp. The motor — 354 cc, SOHC, air-cooled twin — squeezed out an optimistic 31 bhp at 8500 rpm. At that rev limit, it would have been impossible to hear your *Ziggy Stardust* tape, or anything else short of an atomic bomb.

Rob Luck was more complementary in *Wheels,* when he tested a lime-green 'evaluation prototype' model early in 1971. This car made it to the cover of the April 1971 magazine. Luck seemed convinced that when the Z was released in Australia later that year a 600 cc manual version would be available. That would make it a more serious contender in the local market. It would be priced just under the Mini 1100K, according to his maths. 'But even the 360 cc test car was a grabber' wrote Luck. His had twin carbs fitted so put out 36 bhp, a handful more power than the one Ray Bell had tested. Luck's prediction was that the 600 cc version would top 85 mph (137 km/h).

He loved the look of the car too. Fitted with a four-speed manual, he found it ideal for threading through inner city traffic. It was especially suited to taking short cuts down alley ways. He was also impressed by the driving position and the amount of rear luggage space – with access through the distinctive rear window that many compared with the size of a TV screen.

The Japanese always loved the concept of fitting a tiny motorcycle motor into a four-wheel chassis and calling it a car, but the Honda Z was pretty special. It was sporty, it was fun to drive and it appealed to the kind of young buyer who, as shown in the 1972 photos, liked to surf and wear hot pants.

Ray Bell suggested it could also appeal as a shopping trolley for mothers who never left the city limits. 'Handling is in the accepted mini-car, front-wheel-drive tradition,' he wrote, 'the ride is lively, but that shouldn't be too bad, as anyone in their right mind wouldn't take it too far and if they did they would deserve what they got.'

The present writer's recollection is that what they deserved was a car which refused to turn corners in the wet, and liked to roll over on its roof if pushed too hard.

The Z's appeal to collectors today is in its unique design features, which includes a four-speed synchro gearbox operated by a lever mounted on the dash. Fans of the car refer to it fondly as the 'Zot'.

Ampol Trial 1970

A Datsun 1600 SSS driven by Edgar Herrmann with navigator Hans Schuller – who had just come from winning the East Africa Safari – were joint winners of the race that started at Port Augusta and followed a 10,200-kilometre route that took in Alice Springs, Townsville, Brisbane, Adelaide and Melbourne, before finishing in Sydney. Herrmann and Schuller also won the 2000 cc class, a Datsun 1200 driven by Alsion Parker and Carol Wadron triumphed in the women's division, and a standard Datsun 1600 won the novice section. And to cap it off, the tiny Colts won the under-1100 cc class.

1970
AMPOL TRIAL
DRV. MAL LONGMORE
NAV. PETER ROBINSON
100c
AMPOL
AMPOL
AMPOL

Baby Bins

One of the stranger fads of the mid-1970s was the emergence of the mini bins – very small delivery vans, usually powered by tiny two-stroke motors.

Wheels magazine featured one on the cover of their February 1976 edition, which included a 16-page 'Vantastics!' feature story.

Daihatsu, Mazda and Suzuki all had mini vans at the time, although very few were transformed into bonsai sin-bins like the decorated Daihatsu shown on the *Wheels'* cover. The cars were designed in Japan for delivery work in the inner city, although buzzing around in one all day, with that two-stroke screaming away, was a recipe for migraine. These were the main contenders.

- Suzuki L60 V: Price $2550. Front engine, rear drive. 446 cc, two-cylinder, two-stroke. Maximum power, 29 bhp. Sales pitch: 'Boasting a fully trimmed and neatly styled interior with a radio as standard, the van seats two up front and has a useful cargo bay with 500 kg total load capacity.'
- Mazda F1000: Price $2635. Rear engine, rear drive. 987 cc, four-cylinder, OHV. Maximum power, 52 bhp. Sales pitch: 'We've heard the F1000 referred to as the biggest little van on the market and that seems a fair description.'
- Daihatsu 360: Price $2517. Front engine, rear drive. 356 cc, two-cylinder, two-stroke. Maximum power, 26 bhp. Sales pitch: Bigger on the inside than it may seem from the outside, Daihatsu's compact 360 Cab Van is a practical little cargo carrier popular for city and suburban deliveries.'

Despite their limitations, quite a few were sold and they were regularly seen buzzing around cities like automotive bees. Today they are cult cars if you find one that hasn't been thrashed and trashed.

Extra *Special* Corollas

In 1967 Toyota launched the first Corolla in Australia, designated the KE10.

The NRMA's *Open Road* magazine tested the new car in August 1967 and described it as 'an economical and tenacious performer which will carve its own niche in the very competitive under $1,700 market.' Fair call, but would anyone have thought that this car would still be selling in the second decade of the 21st century, after over ten generations of changes?

The Corolla is claimed to be the best-selling car by the biggest car manufacturer in the world. It is the longest running Toyota brand after the Land Cruiser.

Examples from the first KE series are in big demand, especially ones in original condition. Even rarer are the limited-edition Corollas produced by Toyota dealer Bill Buckle in Sydney. The Corolla was already the most popular Japanese car in its class, but Buckle thought a special sports version would be a good marketing concept which would attract younger buyers.

BUCKLE 'S'
TOYOTA
NSW
BB·100
SE

His extra special version was based on the Corolla 1200 SE, modified with a port and polish of the head, a tuned exhaust system with extractor, slight mods to the distributor and carburettor, lower suspension and wider mag wheels. Each car was dyno-tuned and significant increases in horsepower were claimed, making it comparable with a Mini Cooper S. Interior changes included a tape deck and radio, tachometer, and positive action gear shift. A side speed stripe and rear boot panel in black made it stand out from the Corollas in supermarket carparks.

THIS Original series 1967 model Toyota Corolla, still going strong.

NSW
GW-395

Above Third-generation Corolla, late 1970s.

The Corolla specials were available for sale from April 1970, marketed as the Buckle S in Stage 1 or Stage 2 formats. The price was $2280 – $265 above the basic list price for an SE. Existing Corollas could also be converted to Buckle specs. How many were actually sold, and how many survive, is a bit of a mystery, but for early Corolla freaks these are the Holy Grail.

The ultimate Bill Buckle special is the prototype he prepared first. This Corolla was sold in 1969 to Ray Morris who developed it into a serious race machine so that his young son Bobby could learn the art of driving fast – that's the same Bob Morris who went on to win Bathurst in a Torana.

That Corolla prototype was one of two prepared for the new Improved Production regulations for Touring Cars. In Melbourne Dick Thurston had a similar car. Both ran under the corporate banner of Toyota importers AMI. The Ray Morris and Son team was sponsored by Bill Buckle Autos.

Previously, Corollas had dominated the Class A category in Series Production racing but these modified models were something else. At one of its first meetings at Warwick Farm in February

1969, the Morris Corolla surprised everyone by finishing third outright in the main touring car race, admittedly in the wet.

The car Ray Morris bought from Bill Buckle had previously raced at Bathurst in the 1967 Gallaher 500 but was now serving as a test mule for Buckle's 'Corolla S' project. Buckle continued to supply spare parts at mates' rates to Morris. It was already modified with an H&D exhaust system and twin Solex carburettors. Ray Morris replaced the Solex carbs with Webers, then sent the cylinder head and camshaft to Merv Waggott for special treatment while he went to work on the standard suspension, as allowed under the new Touring Car regulations.

New front springs and shockers were made and the rear springs tweaked. A sway bar was added to the front and the rear axle located with radius arms. Drum brakes were replaced by discs. The most obvious external change was a set of 13-inch (33-cm) Minilite mag wheels, plus go-faster stripes along the side. It was claimed to be the fastest production-based Corolla in Australia, possibly in the world.

Meanwhile, on the other side of town, former Mini racer Laurie Stewart was developing his own Toyota dealership in the suburb of Caringbah, with a massive service centre at Miranda. There was some friendly rivalry between the two and Stewart maintained that his dealership sold more Toyotas than Bill Buckle did.

Stewart had already produced his own special Corolla, tricked up with custom paint, mag wheels and a sun roof. He chose the new Celica as the basis for his next special edition. This car was already out-selling competitors like the Ford Capri, Mazda Capella and Fiat 124.

The LS (for Laurie Stewart) 2+2 was launched in mid-1972. Modifications included front and rear spoilers, a 45DCOE

This First-generation Toyota Sprinter.

THIS It would be a long while before a Japanese car won Bathurst outright but early on they were scoring class wins – Toyota had a one-two in Class A in1968.

Weber, modified manifolds and pipes, 6-inch (15-cm) mag wheels fitted with Dunlop SP Sport radials and a rear window louvre, plus dyno tune. This raised the price from $3429 to $4165. Rego was an extra $90.50.

Stewart is unsure how many LS Celicas he actually sold. He says the point of the exercise was to drag in more punters to the showroom where, more than likely, they ended up driving out in a standard car.

Stewart created another very special Celica in 1980. This was the latest model fitted with a turbocharger – and promoted as Australia's first turbo conversion to be declared street legal, with a compliance plate to prove it. It had taken Stewart 12 months, and more than $25,000, to have his turbo Celica approved by the New South Wales Department of Motor Transport. At the media launch, the DMT chief engineer Ray French warned others that modifying a car without approval was illegal.

Stewart announced that he was planning to build up to 100 of the Stewart Turbos over the next year, with the coupe selling for $10,199 and the hatchback for $10,809 – prices that were around $2200 above standard retail prices. A 12-month, 20,000km warranty was included. He claimed that the turbo provided a 77 per

LT
NSW
LS-063

Toyota Corona 1500

LT
LS-063

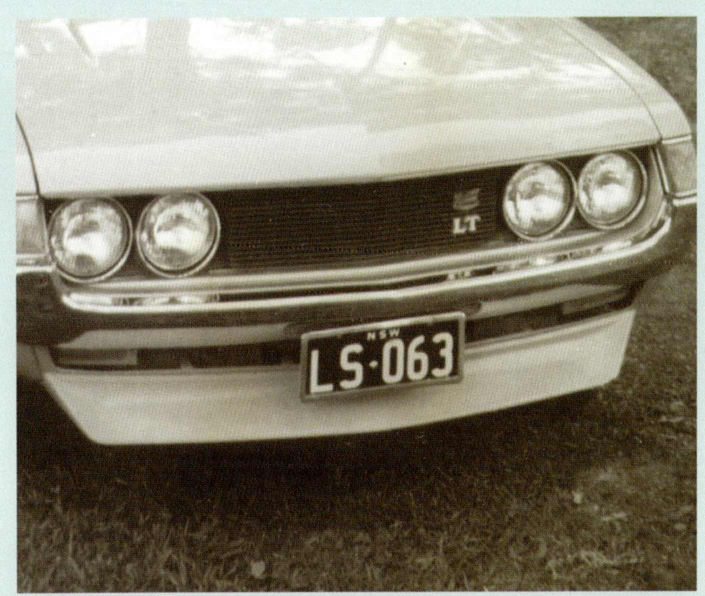

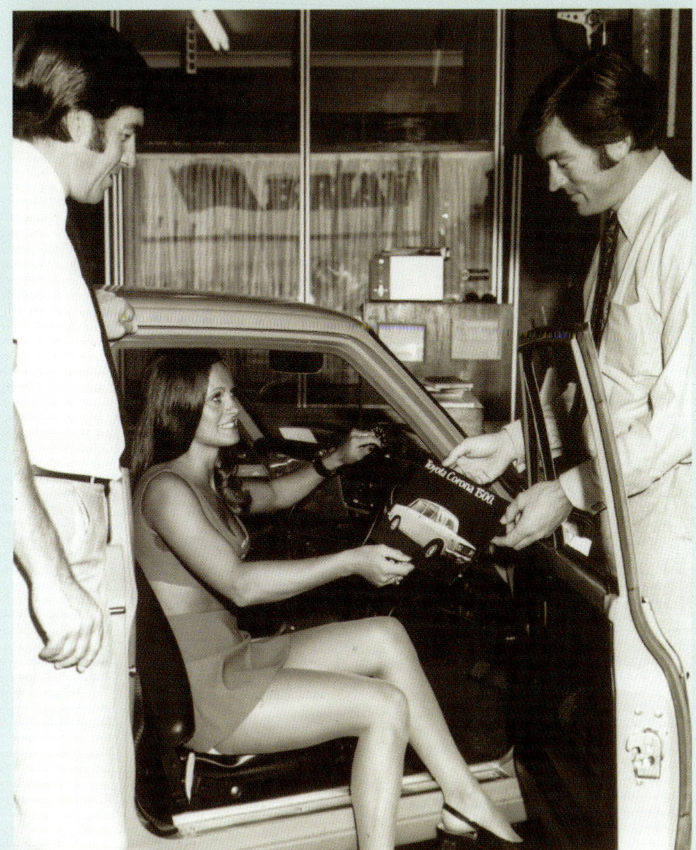

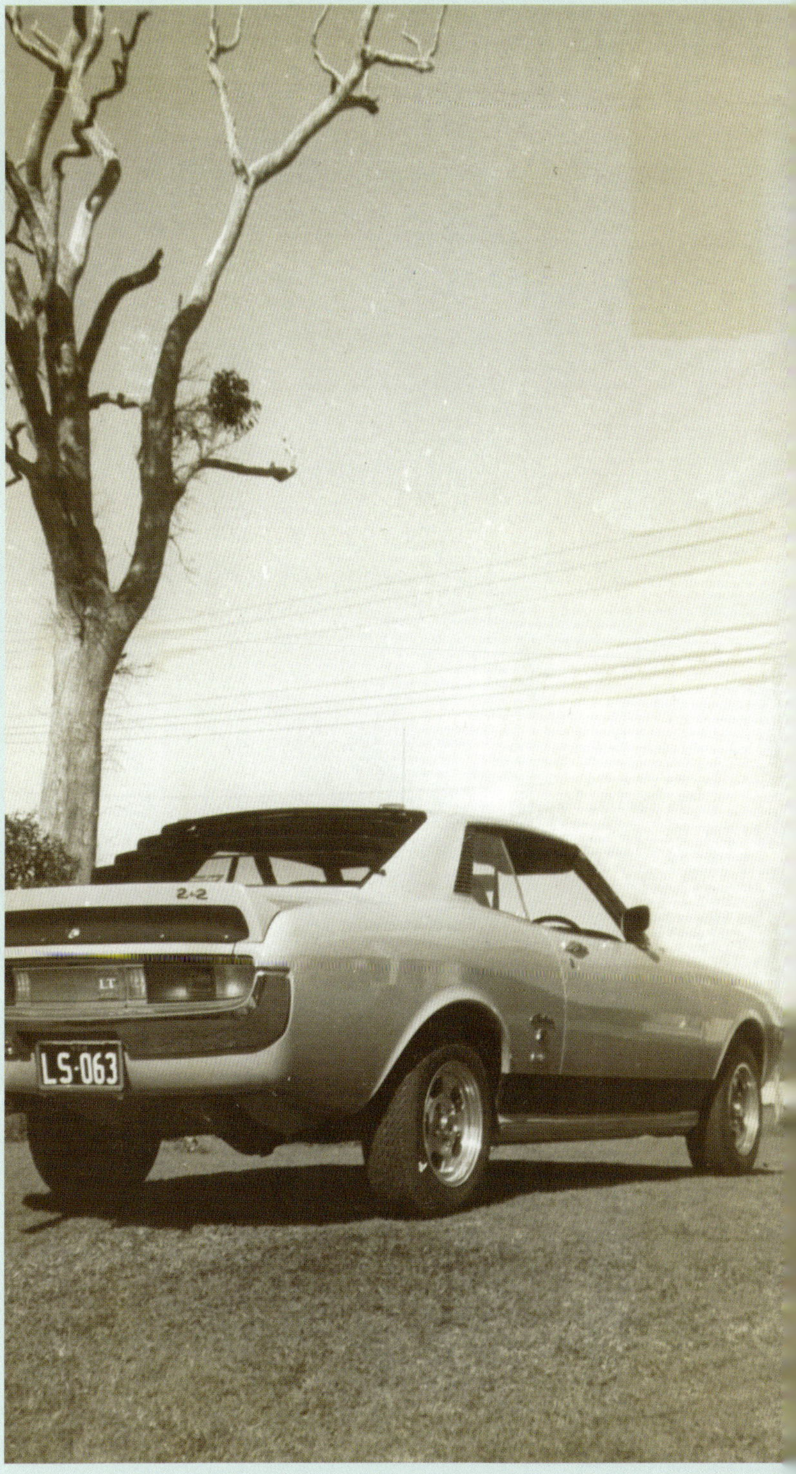

cent increase in power at 3500 rpm. To handle that extra performance, the cars were fitted with a rear stabiliser bar and other suspension improvements.

For Laurie Stewart, who went on to run a taxi business in the Southern Highlands of New South Wales, those special Celicas became distant memories. But he retained a fondness for the turbocharged version. He estimates building around 15 of them and has been told there is one survivor still driving around the streets.

Stewart and Buckle were not the only ones to build specials. In 1980 Peter Wherrett, Australia's best known motoring authority, thanks to his popular *Torque* television series, was after some new challenges. He found one with Mitsubishi, which had recently taken over the Chrysler operation in Adelaide. After a test-drive of their new GH Sigma, Wherrett complained that it was a good basic package but could be a lot better with some minor tweaking.

The response from Mitsuibishi was to offer him a car — and an alleged $50,000 budget — to see if he could improve it: 'a sort of two-way challenge,' as he puts it in his autobiography.

Wherrett commissioned Selby Suspension and K-Mac Engineering to fine-tune the suspension, then asked Sonic Engineering to fabricate a new extractor system. He fitted wider alloy wheels with Pirelli P6 tyres, a pair of Stratos front seats and a Momo steering wheel. The bodywork was re-

painted in red with a black and silver lower panel along the sides.

Mitsubishi were impressed enough by the prototype to agree to build a limited edition of just over a thousand and sell them as Peter Wherrett Specials, complete with his signature on the steering wheel. This series was released in 1981. They had to compromise on a few ideas, and in the end Recaro supplied the front seats, but Wherrett said he was pretty happy with the result. And customers were also happy to buy them.

The Wherrett Specials are sometimes confused with the Sigma Turbo series, which also offered a version in a similar red and black colour scheme.

It takes a lot of car to be more sensational than Sigma.
ANNOUNCING CHRYSLER'S NEW SIGMA SCORPION.
Consider the facts
• 2 Litre Astron Silent Shaft engine
• 5 speed transmission
• Wide, steel belted radial tyres on alloy wheels
• Disc brakes all round
• 4 wheel coil suspension
• Plush velour upholstery
• Soft grip, single spoke steering wheel
• Easy to read instrumentation
• Overhead console with digital clock
• Loop pile carpet
• Pushbutton Radio and Cassette Player
• Fully adjustable seats
• Adjustable tilt steering column
All standard features.
Fully imported from Japan.
At your Chrysler Dealer now.
It's a sensation!

Sigma Makeover

With its unique four-cylinder 'Astron' engine, the late 1970s Sigma was something of a sensation at the time. The Sigma's big point of difference was its unusually large 2.6-litre engine, which used a special twin balance shaft system to reduce vibration and harshness. The Sigma marked the transition from the old Chrysler Australia to the new Mitsubishi Motors Australia — the model was released here as a 'Chrysler' Sigma but before long it became a Mitsubishi.

The Z Factor

Datsun's 240Z was launched in 1969 to rave reviews, becoming the first Japanese sports car to have global sales success. It took off in Australia based largely on word of mouth. Because it would have been beaten in sports car racing by the larger V8s, Nissan chose to promote it mainly through rallying, where its power-to-weight ratio gave it a chance of outright victory.

One of those events was a new concept called the Dulux Rally, in which rally cars competed on a variety of surfaces. For the second rally in 1972, Nissan Australia entered a 240Z driven by Edgar Herrmann, born in Germany, based in Kenya and regarded as an expert at these long-distance marathons. He had won the East African Safari rally twice: in a Datsun 1600 SSS in 1970 and driving a Datsun 240Z the following year. Nissan also entered a Datsun 180B SSS driven by John Roxburgh.

MOTOR CO
Castrol
GTX
GTX
GTX
GTX

IPEC
9
Channel Nine Perth
TRUCK RENTALS
Budget
DATSUN
toms tyres

The two works Datsuns had competed in the Southern Cross Rally earlier that year.

Herrmann was the only international driver to enter the Dulux Rally, which looked like it would be dominated by Peter Brock and Colin Bond, the two Holden Dealer Team stars who were driving the Harry Firth-prepared Torana X-U1s. Bond had won the rally in 1971.

The other notable contender was the veteran racer David McKay, who had managed to convince Ford Australia to import a Ford Capri RS2600 from Germany for him to drive. With lightweight fibreglass panels, it was certainly the fastest machine entered but, as McKay soon found out, was unsuited to the Australian conditions, especially the rougher rally special stages. Other competitors included Paul Older in a BMW 2002, Bob Watson's R12 Renault Gordini, and even a privately entered XW GTHO Falcon.

The Dulux Rally started with a race at Surfers Paradise International Raceway and finished in Melbourne nine days later. On their way down the coast, competitors raced on five race circuits, four hill climbs, one dirt short circuit and several rally special stages, including some held at night. The circuit race at Oran Park was also held under lights. It was seen as a way of bringing the sport of rallying to a wider audience, with strong press and TV coverage. Crowds were healthy.

For many casual spectators, this was

a chance to see a works Datsun 240Z in competition for the first time, driven by one of the world's top professionals. The car was sponsored by Sydney's *Daily Sun* newspaper and Ansett Airlines, which supposedly added a touch of glamour to the Datsun team

Before the event the Datsun was entered in the Surfers Speed Week Concours d'Elegance, with two Ansett hostesses in full uniform as escorts. During the event a couple of Ansett hostesses were in attendance at the start of play each day. The team was especially popular at the regular publicity stops along the route. Huge crowds turned up to see it at shopping centres at Taree and Newcastle.

Unfortunately, it was soon evident that the 240Z was not feeling well. At the first Surfers race meeting the car had an obvious misfire on

right-hand corners, caused by fuel surge. Herrmann initially struggled to keep up with Bond and Brock, who took the lead as expected.

The problem came and went but it was especially severe on the race circuits. It was a source of frustration to Herrmann, who was seen punching the steering wheel of the Datsun as it popped and banged around the fast corners.

He first got to show his skill at the tight Mountainview hill climb at Grafton, where the car had full power and recorded the second fastest time — which was a fraction slower than Colin Bond and a fraction faster than Peter Brock.

When it was on song, the Datsun looked and sounded wonderful.

But the fuel surge returned at the Winton raceway where it had a dramatic consequence. Herrmann had struggled to maintain race speeds on the track and at the end of the race Mini Cooper driver Jon Leighton accused him of intentionally blocking him. Then Leighton punched Herrmann in the face and walked away. Hermann was taken to hospital to have his lip stitched and Leighton was asked to retire from the rally.

Herrmann continued and, with the Datsun behaving better, he began to climb up the leader board after some brilliant driving on the special stages. He was in second place by the final night, but gearbox failure cost him 229 time penalties and he finished fourth, behind the three Toranas of Bond, Brock and the South Australian Stewart McLeod.

Still, Datsun won the unofficial spectator's award for best-looking team, thanks largely to those Ansett hosties.

The Dulux Rally was not held again but the 240Z, and later the 260Z,

DATSUN
DATSUN
3

continued to be a force in Australian rally championships. The top local drivers were McLeod, who swapped to a 240Z soon after the 1972 Dulux, and West Australian Ross Dunkerton.

Ross Dunkerton was the star of the rally scene in his Z cars, winning the Australian Rally Championship in a 240 model in 1975, then the 1976 and 1977 titles in a 260Z. These victories are all the more impressive because Dunkerton was then based in Perth, well away from the traditional rally centres.

Road versions of these cars are among the most desirable of all Japanese classics. The Z series continued with the Datsun 280ZX (introduced in 1979) and the 300ZX (1983, then updated with twin turbos in 1989). The 'X' stands for luxury, but this prefix was dropped for the 350Z (2002) and the Nissan 370Z, the sixth generation of the Z series. These were promoted as a return to the original 240Z sports concept. The 370Z has only two seats and is powered by a 3.5 litre V6 and is bound to be a classic of the future.

Since 1969 over 2 million of Nissan Z series cars have been sold throughout the world, making it the best-selling sports car series ever.

TOYOTA
TOYOTA
1
H.TAKAHASHI
K.MISAKI
Esso
TMSCR

Turbo Prop

Toyota introduced the Celica in 1970 and then spent the next 36 years making it sleeker, faster and even more desirable.While the 1973 turbo (left) turned heads on the racetrack, showrooms full of standard Celicas were attracting more and more satisfied customers.

The Rotary Revolution

December 1978 was a significant moment in Australian car history. That was when Allan Moffat, by then a certified Ford legend, was first approached by Mazda Motors, the Australian arm of Toyo Kogyo based in Hiroshima. He was told that Mazda was keen to get involved in motor racing in Australia with the new Mazda RX7 rotary, which had been launched earlier that year.

There were no deals on the table, no contracts to be signed. The discussion was hypothetical: did he want to be involved? It can be assumed that Moffat thought deeply about the proposal and said yes.

Fast forward to 14 September 1981, to the ballroom of the Hilton Hotel in Melbourne. Allan Moffat, dressed in black tie, presided over what was described as Australia's most spectacular launch of a racing car. This was the first sighting of the Mazda RX7.

Between these two dates ensued a legal and political battle that was worthy of a general election. Mazda Motors had engaged in a long, sometimes bitter, campaign with CAMS to have the RX7 and its radical peripheral port rotary engine approved for racing. As a touring car, not a sports car. After around 20 months of negotiation, it was allowed in the 1981 season.

The RX7 was already racing with some success in Europe and the US. Once committed to the project, Moffat joined an American team to compete at the 1980 Daytona 24-Hour event. He had become a dedicated Mazda man.

Moffat's first Australian race was at Sandown raceway in the last running of the Hang Ten 400. Qualifying nearly three seconds off the pace, he started in 14th position and came home a solid fifth.

It was an excellent debut but nothing for the top V8 teams to lose any sleep over.

At the 1981 Hardie Ferodo 1000 at Bathurst, Moffat qualified 10th for the Hardies Heroes shootout, the first time a non-V8 car had qualified in the Top 10 at

DIE
REBA
FINNIGAN - LEEDS
ACCURATE ENGINE SERVICES
VALVOLINE
CALLAGHAN-GRAHAM
47
LYNX
MACBRO
RENTAL
MOLYBOND
ignis
ignis
McLEOD - BAILEY
50
PETROLON'S
SLICK 50
PERMANENT ENGINE TREATMENT
Valvoline

Mount Panorama. After the shootout, he was on fifth position on the grid.

That was the year a six-car collision at the top of the mountain stopped the race. Based on their positions at the time of the stoppage, Moffat and co-driver Derek Bell were awarded third place – again, the best result ever for a Japanese car.

Competitors in the series then headed directly to Surfers Paradise for the final round of the series. Several of the front runners pulled out and, when Peter Brock's Commodore was penalised a minute for requiring a bump start after a pit stop, Moffat's Mazda was awarded the race victory, the first by a Japanese touring car.

The Mazda RX7 was now a serious contender in Australia's top racing category. The V8 die-hards who followed Touring Car racing with religious zeal were dismayed.

Here was a car that looked like a sports car – there was at best room for a dwarf in the back seat – and was powered by a engine, at first the 12A, with a capacity of 1146 cc. It had one down-draught Weber carburettor, with a claimed power output of 260 bhp. But it sounded like a two-stoke motorcycle or, as some unkindly described it, a sewing machine.

Yet within a few meetings, this strange little car – nicknamed the Hiroshima Screamer – was up there giving the 5-litre V8s a hard time.

Not fair, said the purists.

FEDERAL
MOGUL
Now there's a big
mazda
43
Stuyvesant
INTERNATIONAL
BLUEBIRD
55
NISSAN

Bitupave
the high performance
pavement
...anyhow
Canon
43
Darrell Lea
34
Peter
Stuyvesant
mazda

This Moffat's Mazda gets the short back and sides from Steve Masterton's Falcon at the start of the 1984 Bathurst 1000 (centre right of photo). Luckily Moffat had another RX7 in the race (no 42) which he could swap over to. But it was to be a disappointing day at Bathurst for the Japanese manufacturers.

MASTERTON
2
MASTERTON
HOMES
43
Stuyvesant
JOHNSON FRENCH
BLUEBIRD
15
NISSAN

The Japanese Takeover

Nineteen eighty-three. That was the year the Japanese did what many had thought impossible. They won the Australian Touring Car Championship.

The eight-round series started at Melbourne's Calder Park complex and was expected to be another victory for one of the thundering V8s – Peter Brock in his Marlboro Holden Dealer Team Commodore or Dick Johnson in his Tru-Blu Falcon.

The winner was Allan Moffat in his now-familiar Peter Stuyvesant Mazda RX7 and he went on to drive the car to win the title – the first Japanese car to do so. Moffatt was delighted but was quick to point out that what he was really after was the main event, the James Hardie 1000, the Great Race.

Left No safety car at Bathurst back in the day ... Terry Shiel guides his RX7 around the crash recovery truck.

More surprising at Calder Park was the second placing of George Fury in the Nissan Bluebird turbo, a car still being developed but obviously another serious contender. Prepared by Gibson Motorsport and supported by Nissan Australia, this was the start of an intense eight-year campaign to take over Australian Touring Car racing. The Bluebird finished second in the 1983 series. Peter Brock and Allan Grice in the best of the V8 cars two took rounds apiece.

V8 fans still believed it was impossible for Japanese cars to win at Bathurst – or they did before CAMS announced that Moffat and his growing number of Mazda mates would be allowed to run the more powerful 13B engines. This gave the Hiroshima Screamers an extra 30 horsepower, which they certainly needed when screaming up the mountain lap after lap. To compensate, the V8 drivers were allowed to fit larger wheels and wider rubber.

Guess who won the first two rounds of the Endurance series at Amaroo Park and Oran Park? Fury and his little Nissan won both. Moffat didn't turn up at Oran Park and Dick

Left & opposite The Nissan Bluebird Turbos were very fast at Bathurst but the Japanese were still to figure out how to get their cars to last the 1000 km.

Johnson's larger set of wheels wouldn't fit onto his Falcon when he tried to put them on in the pits.

Before the Castrol 400 race at Sandown, the traditional form guide for Bathurst, CAMS also allowed a fuel-injection system for the 13B rotaries. Before this race, Peter Brock predicted that a Mazda would win at Mount Panorama in October. Moffat was cautious as always, calmly pointing out that the previous year at Bathurst he had been lapped by Brock after only 40 laps.

But at Sandown the impossible happened. Moffat in his enhanced RX7 won after 129 laps. George Fury in his Bluebird was also flying around the power circuit before his turbocharger exploded.

The V8s all had troubles. Bathurst was still being run under Group C regulations. There were 19 Commodores, 13 Falcons, 16 Mazda RX7s and two Bluebirds entered. In the first day of practice, Moffat was dominant in the rain and rally expert George Fury, still in his first full season of circuit racing, qualified second on the grid next to Brock's Commodore.

Brock scored his seventh Bathurst victory, although not without some controversy. He had taken the precaution of driving the second Holden Dealer Team Commodore in practice so when his designated car suffered a bent valve he called in John Harvey and took over his. There were many complaints over the tactic but Peter Perfect had studied the rules and it was legal.

But among all the fuss, it was hardly noticed that Allan Moffat had cruised home to take second place, a lap down on Brock. Another RX7 finished fifth. Fury, who had threatened Brock in the first few laps, suffered gearbox problems.

The Japanese were emerging as serious contenders in Touring Car racing. The bulk of fans who really only cared if Holden beat Ford, or vice versa, suddenly had much more to worry about. Those fans tolerated these cars as long as they stayed in the smaller classes where they belonged. Now it had become only a matter of time before a Japanese car won the big one.

The next year George Fury won pole position in his flying Nissan Bluebird. His practice lap of 2 minutes 13.85 seconds stood as the fastest lap for seven years. This car was soon replaced by a series of increasingly fast Nissan Skylines, also turbo-charged. Garry Scott won pole in one in 1986.

Opposite Nissan went closer than a lot of people think to winning Bathurst in 1987. But Nissan's time would come.
Below Moffat's RX7s showed they could win on any track – except Bathurst.

15
Peter Jackson
Peter Jackson
30
30
Peter Jackson
Peter Jackson
BP Visco
BP Visco
NISSAN
NISSAN

This The factory Nissan Skyline DR30s chase a pair of BMW M3s in the 1987 Bathurst 1000.

NISSAN
Peter Jackson
Peter Jackson
BP Visco
Peter Jackson
30

This The six-cylinder Skyline HR31 was unsuccessful at Bathurst but it would deliver Nissan its first Australian Touring Car Championship title.
Opposite Toyota's Corolla was virtually unbeatable in the baby car class in the late 1980s and early 1990s.

Castrol
DUNLOP
AUSTRALIAN AIRLINES
CRANE Cams
HOLDEN MOTOR SPORT
SCORCHER

PULSAR
16
EXA
NISSAN

Nissan EXA Turbo

Having pioneered the use of turbocharging in Australian touring car racing with the Bluebird model, in 1983 Nissan thought it might be a good idea to run the Nissan EXA Turbo in the under 3-litre class.But it wasn't a good idea.

These were the days before they had fancy viscous diffs and magical computer software to help finesse some 300 horsepower through the front wheels. So, although the little EXA was brutally fast in a straight line, it was just plain brutal all over. Frightening torque steer made it near-undriveable at race speed and – because the boffins decided it wouldn't need power steering – with those big fat front tyres it was also almost undriveable at slow speed.

The steering was so heavy that lead driver Christine Gibson wasn't physically capable of turning the wheel while manoeuvring around the pits – she would have to get out and get one of the Nissan Motorsport mechanics to do it!

On top of all that, the car was hardly a model of reliability – although sometimes when the thing suddenly stopped it was more to the relief of the driver...

'Pack of arseholes' car

The amazing Nissan GT-R R32, aka Godzilla, made its debut late in 1990, driven by Jim Richards and young gun Mark Skaife. At Bathurst that year Richards started in 11th place but had worked his way up to first when the monster died. In 1991 the inevitable happened and Mark Skaife won the race, starting from pole position. Mark Gibbs came in second in a similar Nissan sponsored by GIO.

The V8 fans were not happy chaps.

In 1992 Jim Richards drove the latest spec Godzilla to another victory, sparking the most memorable podium celebration in Bathurst history. The race was stopped on lap 144 when a freak hailstorm flooded the

Payphone
Payphone
wreckair
hire
NISSAN
Winfield
RACING
Shell
wynn's
HIRE

circuit, especially the top of the mountain. Con Rod turned into a fast-flowing river. Richards was in the lead on slick tyres when he slid into the wall, then aquaplaned into some other cars while trying to limp back to the pits. The race was red-flagged and Dick Johnson and John Bowe, parked in the pits at the time, thought they had won. So did the crowd.

Not so. According to the rules, the placings from the previous lap apply when there is a red-flag stoppage.

The Dick Johnson fans assembled at the podium and booed Richards and Skaife when they turned up to collect the trophy. Empty cans were thrown at them. And abuse was hurled.

Jim Richards was visibly upset and told them so. His speech was relayed live over the Seven network, expletives not deleted. 'I'm just really stunned for words,' he said. 'I can't believe the reception. I thought Australian race fans had a lot more to go than this, this is bloody disgraceful.'

He finished with the most famous five words in Australian motorsport: '... you're a pack of arseholes.'

Since then, the 1992 Nissan, run in historic racing by Terry Ashwood, is universally known as the 'pack of arseholes' car. Ashwood is very proud of it. It's also been described as the most hated race car, although now, decades after the event, it has gained a new generation of admirers.

Allegedly the most expensive sedan car in Bathurst history, the Nissan GT-R dominated the final period of Group A racing and led to a total revamp of the Touring Car regulations to make racing closer and cheaper.

In fact, the Nissan is a technological marvel, unique to Australia, complete with a four-wheel-drive system masterminded by

Gibson Motorsport. The car would start in rear-wheel-drive mode, then switch to 4WD once in motion. It would then adjust itself according to track and weather conditions. In 1992 the car also had a unique ballast system fitted, the result of CAMS giving the car a weight handicap in the manner of horse racing. Fred Gibson placed some of the required lead pellets – around 200 kilos worth – inside the rear cross-member where it would little impact. The extra weight slowed the car down but only just.

Some were relieved when Nissan pulled out of the championship at the end of 1992; others admit they miss the drama – and podium speeches – of this volatile period.

Gibson Motorsport Nissans are among the most sought-after Japanese cars made in Australia, including one that seems to have slipped under the radar.

NSC·389

Toyota 86

In the late 1980s Mazda reimagined a 1960s British four-cylinder open-top sports car, but built using modern technology. The MX5 was a fantastic little sports car in the style of the classic 1960s Brits, with Japanese build quality and reliability. Mazda suddenly had a mortgage on a market segment the rest of the automotive world hadn't bothered with for years. Mazda couldn't sell enough of the things, and today the MX5 lineage continues – it's now a classic in its own right.

In the 2000s Toyota did something similar. Identifying that no-one was offering a low-cost/high-fun, front-engined rear-wheel drive GT-style coupe, Toyota got together with Subaru and came up with the 86.

The 86 name is in recognition of the mid-1980s AE86-model Corolla, the last rear-wheel drive Corolla and one that became the weapon of choice for thousands of drivers who indulge in the made-in-Japan sport

of drifting. Naturally the 86 caught the undivided attention of the drifting world, but its appeal stretches far further.

Since its release, it has become a cult classic. In Sydney the 'Festival of 86' attracted over 800 Toyota 86/Subaru BRZ (the Subaru version) fanatics. Half the punters were Toyota 86 owners, and there were another 50 AE86 Corolla owners. The car's global chief engineer, Tetsuya Tada, attended and he was mobbed, spending most of the time signing everything from car components to scale-models, T-shirts, owner manuals and posters.

Just as the 86 coupe has proven an international phenomenon, it is a lot more than just a modern version of the last Corolla that was fun to drive. The car's heritage goes back a lot further: there's a distinct styling resemblance to Toyota's 1960s sports coupe, the 2000GT.

#FESTIVALOF86
LIVE
Black Magic
Hypertune
SEIBON
NITTO
GEARWRENCH
Wynn's
SHAWFIRE.com.au
GCG
Hypertune
NITTO
Achilles

Mazda Conquers Mount Panorama

After Moffat's success with the Mazda RX7, a later version of the car also dominated the series of endurance races known as the Bathurst 12-Hour.

A Toyota Supra won the first event in 1991, then Mazda Australia decided this was a good promotional opportunity and entered a pair of their new Series 5 cars in the 1992 race. The Mazda team of Charlie O'Brien, Garry Waldon and Mark Gibbs won the race, with John Bowe and Gregg Hansford finishing fifth that year in the second works car.

T
17
mazda
JAMES HARDIE
12 HOUR
Arai
mazda

TOYOTA
2
MR2
STICKS LIKE GLUE
Castrol
DUNLOP
DUNLOP
DUNLOP

Alan Jones and Garry Waldon teamed up to win in 1993, with O'Brien and Hansford in second place, two laps behind. Hansford and Neil Crompton won in 1994. In 1995, when the 12-Hour race was relocated to Eastern Creek, Dick Johnson and John Bowe won again in another Mazda.

Because the cars in these events had to be production-based with limited modifications, the RX7s were kept as close to showroom condition as possible.

In 1993 Todd Hallenbeck tested one of the team cars at Oran Park for *Fast Fours and Rotaries* magazine and was surprised to see just how close to standard they were. The car he tested was the one driven by Jones and Waldon when they won that year's race (it had also been used in the 1992 race).

In 1992 the cars had competed within three weeks of arriving in Australia and had had a minimal amount of preparation: 'what amounted to a wash and tyre pressure check before the race,' noted Hallenback. For 1993, the motors were pulled down and given new seals and bearings but the rotors and turbos were the same ones used the previous year.

Left While Mazda took top honours in three of the four Bathurst 12-Hour in the 1990s, Toyota's MR2 was king in the smaller capacity classes.

Both cars ran with top-of-the-range options available in all RX7s sold in Australia. These included power windows and mirrors, air con, cruise control and, yes, a sun roof. The spoiler kit fitted was standard. Five-speed manual and ABS were also standard, as were the coil springs on the double A-arm independent suspension, front and rear.

A few journos criticised the firm ride of the street cars, claiming it was closer to a race set up.

For the Series 5, the Mazda 13B rotary had been given minor modifications, notably a primary 54-mm turbined turbo plus a secondary 50-mm unit. Boost was electronically controlled through the ECU, which opened and shut the single wastegate. Max boost was 13 psi, with a maximum output of 136 kW at 6500 rpm. This proved to be a nice balance between top speed and endurance.

Several other Japanese high-performance cars were entered in the series of Bathurst 12-Hour races, including the Honda NSX, Nissan Skyline GT-R, and Toyota MR2, but none could challenge the RX7 for outright honours around Mount Panorama.

The *Cult* of WRX

For a long while Subaru in Australia was seen as that other Japanese manufacturer with its quirky four-cylinder boxer engine – kind of like a water-cooled VW Beetle engine. If you wanted to own a Japanese car and still feel as though you had something that was different, then Subaru was for you.

But increasingly into the 1990s, Subaru was for you not so much if you wanted to be different, but very much so if you wanted to go fast. The late 1980s Liberty/Legacy model showed that Subaru was quite capable of building a 'normal' medium-sized sedan, and the turbo versions demonstrated Subaru also knew how to build one that was quick.

But although the Liberty RS was certainly a fast machine, it was the introduction of the Impreza model and its performance variant, the turbo all-wheel-drive WRX, which changed the game. Those three initials which today virtually define the term high-

WRX

performance all-wheel drive turbo sedan (the same can be said of the three initials of its arch-enemy, the 'EVO') originally stood for World Rally eXperimental, which shows the WRX's heritage as a rally vehicle.

Of course, in the forests it didn't disappoint, both here and on the world stage. From 1995 on, between the late Possum Bourne and Cody Crocker, the WRX would win the Australian Rally Championship ten years in a row.

More than 20 years and several Impreza model generations on and the WRX is a motoring institution in its own right.

In Australia it's achieved cult status: a car with supercar-type performance that looks cool, and at a price within reach of most 20-somethings.

Datsun Baby, Reborn

The growing interest in Japanese classic cars also applies to the manufacturers. Nissan is especially proud of its own history, no matter how small.

In April 2015 a restored Datsun Baby - or Honda Z - was put on display at Nissan's Yokohama headquarters to celebrate the 50th anniversary of the opening of the popular theme park Kodomo no Kuni (Children's Land) near Tokyo. The display vehicle is one of 100 specially-made children's cars designed and built by Nissan in 1964/65 for use at the Kodomo no Kuni. Each car was given its own numberplate.

The design was based on the Cony Guppy, a 200 cc two-passenger utility truck from

the Aichi Machine Industry Company. The Datsun Baby features a four-wheel independent suspension system with double wishbones at the front, automatic transmission, a speed limiter that kicks in at 30 km/h and working headlights. The futuristic body style was inspired by sports car design of the time. The car has been restored without the protective bars used at the park.

The project captures a unique part of Japanese culture — the cute factor — evident in everything from the sushi train to fads like Hello Kitty and manga comics. The Datsun Baby, or Honda Z, is as significant as a Falcon Phase III is in Australia.

Nissan Returns

The biggest news of 2013 was the return of Nissan to Australian motorsport. The revival was part of the V8 Supercars' Car of the Future policy, which was designed to encourage other manufacturers to join the Holden-Ford only category.

Nissan was close to last on the list of potential candidates. For a start they didn't have a suitable car in their range. Then they announced that the Nissan Altima, front-wheel drive and powered by a four or six cylinders, would be the donor vehicle. This meant converting the design to rear-wheel-drive and transplanting the V8 from its Nissan Patrol.

The Altima body, more aerodynamic that Holden's or Ford's, had to be modified to achieve parity. Some noted that the only resemblance to the Altima you would find in the showroom was the Nissan badge on the grille.

Nissan Australia sales executive director Ian Moreillion, who spearheaded the concept, handed the project over to Kelly Racing to make it happen. Rick Kelly and his team had around four months to build and test four cars before the season began. A big call by anyone's standards.

Still, the media seemed to love the concept, pointing out that this was the same manufacturer that had quit Australian motorsport when the V8 Supercar formula began. Now it was making a comeback after 20 years. Jimbo's 1992 'pack of arseholes' quote appeared in just about every story, as did nostalgic images of the Nissan GT-R in its glory days.

The question was, could Nissan revive any of that magic? The cars looked great in the publicity photos, painted black with impressive sponsorship from Jack Daniel's, Harley-Davidson and Mack trucks. The Nissan name featured prominently on the front, so that old-school spectators would know that this was a Japanese car and give it heaps.

As predicted, the new Nissans were less impressive on the track – which was only to be expected for a brand-new team created on such short notice. Over the season Rick Kelly performed best of all four Nissan drivers, finishing 14th overall.

But just as the naysayers were starting to write the obituaries, Nissan struck gold at Winton, one of the less populated locations in the national series. Here James Moffat, son of the legendary Allan, scored the first win for Nissan in the modern era. His team-mate Michael Caruso came second in the race, one of three held that weekend.

Nissan gained great publicity from their one-two finish – an impressive start to the return of Godzilla.

LIQUI MOLY
35A
NISMO
nismo
NISSAN
nismo
35A
ICOM
NISSAN
nismo
MICHELIN
MOTUL

Godzilla LIVES!

Japanese cars might have a chequered history in the Bathurst 1000, but it's been a different story in the Bathurst 12-Hour production car races. But in 2011 when they changed the rules to allow in GT3 sports cars, they looked certain to fail.

The 12-Hours held in the 1990s were all won by Japanese cars – Toyota Supra in 1991, Mazda RX7 Twin Turbo in 1992, 1993 and 1994. When the race was reborn in the 2000s, once again the Japanese cars generally showed the Euros a clean pair of heels – that is, except in the two years when BMW's 335i won.

But in 2011 they changed the rules and opened it up to exotic GT3 sports cars. This was a problem: as fast a car as Mitsubishi's Lancer Evo 10 is, it isn't in the same street as your average Ferrari or Lamborghini.

In a flash, the previous year's leading contenders had been reduced to merely making up the numbers. The switch to GT3 seemed to spell the end for Japanese cars in long-distance races at Bathurst.

Or so it seemed. One of the manufacturers involved in GT3 sportscar racing was Nissan, and for the 2014 race it decided to send one of its GT3-modified GT-Rs out for the 12-Hour. It didn't go well, the GT-R making an early exit after unwanted contact with the wall.

Undeterred, they returned for 2015 with Japanese driver Katsumasa Chiyo, German Florian Strauss and Belgian Wolfgang Reip. Wolfgang had earned his place on the squad via the novel means of winning Nissan's Playstation gaming competition, but whatever comparative lack of actual real racing experience he had, it didn't seem to show on the track.

Against the most competitive field yet in the race, the Nissan hung in there and

managed to jump the leading Audi R8 right at the end to score a memorable victory.

So it was that 22 years after the original Nissan GT-R 'Godzilla' was banned from Bathurst, its newest descendent returned to claim another GT-R victory on the Mountain.

NISSAN
NISSAN
nismo
NISSAN
nismo
MOTUL
ICOM
MICHELIN
ICOM
MOTUL
NISSAN
35A
RCHEAP

A Mazda *with* Elan

The Mazda MX5 sports car was a sensation when it was released in 1989. It's still going strong today; in fact, it's one of the world's most loved cars, a real global motoring icon.

The origins of the MX5 go back as far as 1976. The story goes that the idea for the car came out of a conversation between then motoring journalist Bob Hall and Kenichi Yamamoto and Gai Arai, who ran Mazda's R&D department.

What type of car should Mazda build, they asked Hall? The kind of simple, classic open-top British sports car that doesn't exist any more, Hall replied.

Five years on and Yamamoto had risen to become chairman of Mazda, while Hall had packed away his typewriter and taken a positon in Mazda USA's product planning position. Some time in 1982 the pair remembered their conversation from five years earlier.

There began the MX5 project.

Hall's idea of a modern version of a classic British sports car is clearly evident in the design and layout of the original MX5 - rear-drive, front-mounted twin-can four cylinder engine, light weight, space for two adults and no more. Just like an old MG (or even the old Datsun 2000 Fairlady, which was, even if it was hard to admit at the time, an all-round better car than the classic MGB) or even a 1960s Lotus Elan. In fact, you don't need to look too closely at the 1989 model MX5's shape to see the clear Lotus Elan styling references. And

that really sums up the original MX5: a modern-day Lotus Elan but with Japanese build quality and reliability.

Coincidentally, at around the same as the MX5 was released, Lotus brought back their own Elan model. But the new Elan, with its dowdy styling and – to Lotus fans' horror – front-wheel-drive layout, was a like sad parody of the original 1960s Elan.

No doubt some of the folk at Lotus would have looked at what Mazda had done with the MX5, and come to the realisation that the Japanese had built the very car Lotus should itself have built.

This Drawing inspiration from the great British sports cars of the 1960s, Mazda has created an ongoing legend of its own in the MX5.

A Rockpool book
Published by Rockpool Publishing
PO Box 252 Summer Hill
NSW 2130 Australia
www.rockpoolpublishing.com.au
www.facebook.com/RockpoolPublishing

First published in 2015

National Library of Australia Cataloguing-in-Publication entry

Turning Japanese : 60 years of Japanese motoring in Oz.
9781925017755 (paperback)
Automobiles, Foreign–Australia.
Automobiles–Japan–History.
Automobile industry and trade–Australia.
Automobile industry and trade–Japan.
338.7629222

Cover design by Ben Hay
Internal design by Ben Hay and Como Street Gang
All images by Chevron Publishing Group, a division of Nextmedia, except p33 (main) jeremyg3030, pp62-63 Nordhornerll, p128 Luc106
Typeset by Como Street Gang
Printed and bound by China
10 9 8 7 6 5 4 3 2 1